There's a story that my mother told...

There's a story that my mother told.....
.....so I know it to be true

It's of a horse, kind brave and bold, I'll tell the tale to you
Discharged from the army, with a brand upon his chest
He'd seen the bloody battles put the Kaiser to his rest
All sorts of contraptions he had been shackled to
He'd lost an eye in the Dardenells and in Boxford lost a shoe

Now the Pattle boys u'd ride bare back as they travelled horses round
Came up the farm one frosty morn, a buyer to be found
From the Garrison the old man said 'twas where these horses came
"So what price the one he did enquire whose poor as a crow and lame"
"Not much" said old Bill Pattle "almost anything'll do"
For he's lost an eye in the Dardenells and in Boxford lost a shoe

So we took him in and fed him up, dressed his feet and combed his mane
And with some loving kindness, he came back to life again
One day the old man rode him out and he came back with a smile
He'd galloped down to Kersey Bell and back, it's about 3 mile
When we asked him what to call him, he just said Sparks 'll do
For he's lost an eye in the Dardenells and in Boxford lost a shoe

He won at Tendring Hundreds and when the old man rode him home
He jumped the queech, a mighty gap, where none before had gone
He was the talk of the hunting field and to prove I tell no lies
Just read the sporting columns of The East Anglian Daily Times
And when the old man rode him out, there was always such to do
For he'd lost an eye in the Dardenells and in Boxford lost a shoe

One day there was a dreadful fire and the old man wept full sore
Old Sparks he won't come out his box, he was gone for ever more
But no skin we gave to the huntsman, or body for his hounds
He was laid to rest by Justice Wood, his happy hunting grounds
We chose the spot most carefully, not any where would do
For he'd lost an eye in the Dardenells and in Boxford lost a shoe

The above song was sung by Andrew Stannard in the narrative Ruby and her Horses that we performed together in the years 2006, 2007 and 2008 in village halls across Suffolk and other counties. The stories contained here in are an extension of that narrative and this book has been published to a large extent at the request of these audiences who received the songs and stories so well.

There's a story that my mother told...

true life stories told in the latter part of her life by Ruby Lanham from her experiences in the agricultural depression of the 1920s and 1930s

Edited by Neil Lanham

photoset by George Lanham

There's a story that my mother told...

true life stories told in the latter part of her life by Ruby Lanham from her experiences in the agricultural depression of the 1920s and 1930s

Edited by Neil Lanham

photoset by George Lanham

Almost all pictures shown here were taken by Ruby in the period or were part of her collection. Where pictures have been used from other sources credits are shown. I am indebted to a number of people for their help particularly Prof. John Widdowson, Roy Brazier, Pat Dobel, Katrina Eady, my sister Audrey Lanham, Jan Ralling, Tim Plumridge, Fony Whymark, and my son George who toiled under my idiosyncrasies to do the print setting and to Paul Marsh for cleaning and enhancing a number of Ruby's photos; the late Pat Freeman and Elizabeth Gardiner (Muriel Rainsford's daughter) for various additional photographs.

To my mother Ruby Lanham whose stories shaped my life

Front cover: Ruby standing on the back of Blossom
Rear cover: Ruby riding the pedal roller by ASF Robinson

First published in 2007 by
Traditions of Suffolk
Traditionsofsuffolk.com
Ivy Todd, Helions Bumpstead, Nr Haverhill, Suffolk, CB9 7AT
01440 730414

ISBN 978-0-9555947-0-0

Edited by Neil Lanham

photoset by George Lanham

The Ballad of Maria Marten and the Red Barn Murder

Come all you thoughtless young men a warning take by me
For Monday next is to be my last I'm to be hang'ed from a tree
My name is William Corder a name you know quite well
Brought up by honest parents and the truth to you I'll tell

I went unto her father's house on the 13th day of May
Saying come my dear Maria we'll name the wedding day
I'll meet you at the Red Barn and as sure as I have life
I'll take you up to Ipswich Town and there make you my wife

So with heart so light and thought so gay to meet him she did go
He murdered her all in that barn and laid her body low
Now all things being silent her spirit could not rest
She appeared unto her mother who suckled her at breast
Her mother's mind being so disturbed when she dreamt it three
times oer
That her daughter she lay murdered beneath the Red Barn floor

Her father went unto the barn and when he there did thrust
He found his daughter's body a mingling with the dust
My trial was hard I could not stand woeful was my plight
The sight when her jaw bone was brought to prove which pierced
my heart quite

Adieu to you my loving friends, my race is almost run
For Monday next is to be my last from the gallows I'll be hung
So you young men who do pass by a pity take on me
For murdering Maria Marten I was hang'ed from a tree.

Sung by Sidney Turkentine of Bulmer Tye.
Ted Marten and a lot of Maria's descendants used to work
at Red House Farm.

My father Charles Alleston ready for market. We always called him 'the Old Man'

Introduction by Neil Lanham

Over several mornings in the winter of 1995, I asked my mother Ruby to repeat to me the stories from her life that she had told us as children. These she told me one after the other just as if it were yesterday, taking us back to the point in time. Some I had heard many times, others I had not heard at all. During my lifetime I had thought about mother and her stories many times. As a boy I would go down to the cartlodge when the farm men were having their breakfast and listen to their tales, I would go back and tell mother things that had been said, she in turn would then tell me similar stories of when as a girl, she had been down the cartlodge with the men at their breakfast and other meal times. I did not however realise quite how important these stories were, not for the information that they passed but how they formed my mind in being able to see principles of understanding for that, I have come to realise, is what the sharing of experiences does. I wrote my thoughts in an article for Storylines, the magazine for the **Society of Storytellers** which I repeat here from when it was published in September 2003.

Experience Teaches Wisdom

When the Sporting Life on 15th October, 1994, carried a profile on the Newmarket Racehorse Trainer, Geoff Pearce, he stated that the person who had given him the impetus to get going, was Mrs Ruby Lanham, then aged 88. Ruby Lanham, my mother, was born Ruby Alleston on 27th December, 1905, at Bures, Suffolk, and she was the eldest of four. Sadly she died on 7th February, 1998.

Friends, acquaintances and others would travel many miles to visit mother, who they said was a character. When I think about it now I realise that they did not say she was a character because she told jokes, played pranks, or because of the way she looked but because she simply sat and told stories: stories from her life, and stories from others who had in turn told her stories from their lives - all from living memory - nothing out of books.

I can hear people, who had suffered bereavement, saying that mother had helped them and likewise those with problems, financial or otherwise. She would 'hold court' at hatchings, matchings and despatchings (christenings, weddings and funerals) with people hanging onto her every word as she related stories from the past, punctuating them with 'howsomiver', constantly taking the part of all the various players in the adventure with dialogue 'So I said to him...' and 'He said to me...' It seemed no problem for her to convert an adventure into a story, in fact she could not tell it otherwise. She did not approve of reading books, well novels at any rate. She felt they were a waste of time. Yet she was a mine of information, and what she did not know she knew where to find or who to get it from. She, of course, had a Cookery Book but the recipes were handwritten by herself that she had gathered from people around her. It included everything from her grandmother's pickle for Suffolk Sweetcure Hams to homemade Cough Mixture, Linseed Tea, or 'Hoss Oil' embrocation – all handed down and all to be used.

She hated stories of fairies and dragons and things that she could not believe in. I believe that this was because she thought that they could not be true, and were subversive to the truth that mattered so much to her. This, from a person who was exceedingly superstitious – we were never allowed to say 'goodbye' only 'cheerio' or 'farewell' and she would always kiss the gatepost when arriving home from a long journey. I think that this was her way of recognising the enormous amount of chance that lies in life and all we do. Furthermore, having worked with old Horsemen, she would tell of their belief in the witchcraft of charming horses with frog's bone, milch, and secret oils. When my sister, Audrey, was born with cats fur across her face (mother had put her hands on her face whilst carrying Audrey when a cat was killed on the road) mother knew that the only way to be rid of it was to rub a little of her own spittle on it night and morning, which she did and it went. She told us of this and how she had learned it, together with a good many more 'non-medical' cures, from Granny Griggs, the old village midwife. She had seen ghosts and was a strong believer in their presence.

I cannot think of a single storybook that we had as children and we certainly were not read stories at bedtime, so you may think that we had a deprived childhood. Not so, we may have been as 'poor as church mice' but we were as 'rich as sheenies' in stories – stories of 'shared experience' being told all the time and everywhere, but mostly at mealtimes. They were never told for the sake of telling a story, but always with a practical interest appertaining to a situation in hand, passing wisdom on from the truth of experience learned from the harsh realities of life. Many of mother's stories were about horses and often from the hard days in agriculture of the late 1920s, early 1930's. A time she would say when 'If you hadn't got anything boy, you were lucky because you did not have to worry about it, for sooner or later as sure as god made little green apples you would lose it'. These stories of no money, eating from table and chairs with the bailiffs stickers on them, passed on a sense of occasion, thrift, appreciation, place, belonging, opportunity and more. She was sharing the experiences of life and in it passing on lessons of wisdom through conversation rich in imagery.

In the early 1960's a friend took me to the first Cambridge Folk Festival. A young group, 'The Watersons', sung a song that I was sure I had heard mother sing, but how could she have seen books on folk songs, I thought, or heard any folk records. 'The 'old goat' cannot possibly know any folk songs' I thought. I was of course wrong and very wrong. She did know them, but they were never called folk songs. Sometime later, after much persuasion, she came out with the best part of three verses of this song 'When first I went a waggoning' and a lot more traditional songs in fragments, all learned off people around her and passed on by word of mouth in the true oral tradition. Like most other people I thought if it was not in a book then it could not be 'proper' and the same with stories. It took me a long while to realise that these were traditional songs and that the tradition, in its ever-changing form, still goes on around us all the time. It took me even longer to realise that we each have our own tradition that is represented within us by all that we have inherited and been influenced by since the cradle, or even before. It is our culture. Collectively it can be the culture of the area that we were brought up in or even of a nation. I had to get away from the false notion that education

– well education of the academic sort - had instilled into me that books come first before I could see the truth of the fuller world. Everything is firstly about people. Stories come from people, and stories that are committed in written words to paper have all come firstly from people, and then are mostly written into books by a third party with an external perception of the culture they portray. Stories are all around us everywhere and just waiting to be made up as they always have been. The Tradition is ongoing. It can be our own culture or it can be a culture witnessed in others.

When my father died I was five, and my Uncle Tickles took me under his wing on a farm, which had no electricity, only hand-pumped water and external sanitation. He had hardly ever been off the farm but, like all 'long headed men', had an acute awareness of the things around him. He was, by his own admission, 'As sharp as a bag of chisels' and 'As artful as a wagon load of monkeys'. He would be down the Cart Lodge on a Monday morning with the men when they were having their breakfast, where he would get the gossip, then tell it to us at breakfast, embroidering it with expressions of imagery. Then if he thought that the tale was good enough, by the time he went down to his local pub on a Thursday night, it would come out as a yarn and, if he liked it, it would be filed in his head for years to come to make a point or a truism - all with humour. Similarly he made his own songs from local occasions as he rode the tractor, all from experiences. Like his 'R-tomic Drillman', 'Three dows flew from the creach (three pigeons flew from a spinney with a watercourse running through it)', 'Pig feeding calypso', 'When you are awfully light on the trigger' inspired by a dose of the 'backyard trots' during the blackberry season. All put together in the same way as his stories – with an eye to the humorous telling of the story. More important than his stories were the strange little sayings that he used to come out with. When I think about them now they did not just pass on information but an ability to see things from a different angle and above all they passed on the ability to correlate. They were not just rhymes about the weather or crops, but, principles of understanding. He would come out with things like 'Old dogs for hard roads and a lean dog for a bitch'. If a young woman got into trouble, or someone else's wife had gone off or there was going to be a wedding or something like that then you can bet that in all this gossip that a thin fellow would be involved, and he would say 'Told you boy. Lean dog for a bitch' or 'An old dog for hard roads' if an old stayer had triumphed over adversity. He used descriptions like 'Cold enough this morning boy for a suit of sleeved weskits' or 'Cast in yer box' (as when a horse gets down and cannot get up) if you were late getting up in the morning. If he wanted you to get on he would say 'Get for'rad Mrs Gorrod, the cart hang' and who can fail to see the mental image of a fat lady in the back of a tilting cart, or 'You can hang round a long time, boy, with your mouth open before roast chicken fly in' and 'It is not what you know but it's knowing what you don't know, boy, that counts'. He'd make it sound muddled up on purpose to make you think but it gave you the all important imagery. If you asked something that you should not he would say 'Can you keep a secret... well so can I!' When we were young he would keep asking us about our learning. 'If a herring and a half cost a penny and a half, how many do you get for a shilling?' It taught you to look at things in a different way and to correlate information – figures – measured information into useable wisdom. A recent Storyteller said that 'It encapsulated the gathered wisdom of centuries' and I believe that it did. Stories were passed the same whether for adults or children alike as long as you were 'seen and not heard!' you could listen and you were expected to.

He would use local words that you will not find in national or even Suffolk word dictionaries, like 'dinge', 'dag', 'hazeling', 'sludder' and would even make up his own words as he went along to give better communication to colleagues. As that great wordsmith, Adrian Bell, said 'My education only began when I had the privilege of listening to the prowess of expression of Suffolk farm men in their stories', and George Ewart Evans that champion of 'from mouths of men' said similar.

What of legends. They did not come from literature or any printed matter but were orally told of local people, such as Ernie Nunn, the huntsman, who 'Had enough skill with hounds to draw them off when in full cry', something that allegedly no others had. Or Lightning Lock, the Scrapman, who was of traveller extraction, very tall and who had an extraordinary reach and would stand on the hill at Long Melford on a Saturday night and take anyone on bare fist for a pound. Tales of him grew larger and larger – it was alleged that when he fought the Russian at Sudbury they had to take the roof off the Town Hall to get all the people in.

What of myths. Decisions about the countryside are mostly taken by people outside of the community that they are to be levied upon. An academic student, or a 'damn learned scientific man' would be given a hard time – because all they had was information and not the experience to use it wisely - the experience that can only come by doing the job. 'It is only book knowledge' they would say, 'Only book knowledge', and tales would follow how such people had 'Come a cropper'. Of course books are a source of reference for information but it is experience that counts, experience from life. Oral Tradition is experience. The correlation of experience is wisdom.

I recently heard the storyteller Jane Grell and was much impressed by the way that she exhibited her Caribbeaness. Tickles was just the same and would put all of his culture into what he did. Our speech with its imagery, our background, our self, our culture is a very important part of our stories. They may be just 'reminiscences' to those people from outside 'collecting' oral history as academic information and, of course, not everyone is a storyteller, but there are still a good many natural storytellers around in rural areas - where the tradition of song and storytelling has survived at its strongest.

All of this is so well explained by Jack Zipes in the society booklet 'The Storyteller Revisited'. It concerns essays written in 1936 by that extraordinary man Walter Benjamin, whose mind was as clear as a bell as to what storytelling represents. It concerns the exchange of experience in which one learns something about ones self and in doing so passes on wisdom to others. 'Counsel woven into the stuff of lived life is wisdom' he said. 'Storytelling is all around us and a genuine storyteller is by necessity a subversive'.

The best book that I have read about the countryside is that written by a farmworker in his old age and is made by his non 'literacy'. Lilas Rider Haggard, who edited it, had the good sense

*to keep in his imagery by way of expressions, his words and his
tongue. It is an important book because it is one of the very few
written from an internal perspective of it's culture and that makes
all the difference. On page 181, of the 'Rabbit's Skin Cap', you
will find the author's words - written himself from his oral
tradition - 'Experience teaches wisdom'.*

This will give you some idea of the thoughts that came from
the interesting voyage of discovery that Ruby's stories started
me on.

Having got mother to record her stories onto a taperecorder I
asked Pip Harding who was to type them not to change one
word as I wanted it firstly written as she said it and not in the
ways of primarily 'standard' English. Prior to this I had read
what Walter Ong had written so I did not want my mother's very
personal speech transformed by unnecessary modernisms for
'writing transforms thought' said Ong.

Yet when I lent the draft to an author who had had work
published to read for me it came back altered. I particularly
noticed that the word 'that' that she had regularly used, had
been substituted many times for 'it'. Her techniques of repeating
and using short sentences and saying things that seemed back to
front had also been altered. I altered it back to how it is here for
I feel that the way she spoke is vital to the understanding of the
stories and the whole ambience of the times that go with them.
In telling Professor John Widdowson, the former head of the
Folklife Department at Sheffield University how she constantly
used the word 'that' instead of 'it', he said this is old English - pre
Norman - Saxon English. This is the area of the Saxons, they
ruled this land a thousand years ago. We all have our identity
that is carried deep within us. This is passed by the spoken
word said Walter Ong. We are all born into orality, the world of
the spoken word and start to take our identity from our mothers.
I had heard other rural people speak in the same way before but
the thought that our identity could have been passed down to us
through a thousand years made the hair stand on the back of my
neck. Walter Ong in his excellent book Orality and Literacy
(translated into 12 languages) tells us that we need to re-examine

our identity and the subject to do that with is the difference between orality and literacy. The quest that Ruby had sent me on led me to realise that not just our personal identity but our regional and even national identity is passed solely by the spoken word (orality) and with it all of our traditional cultures and regional trades and furthermore the great debt that we owe to the vernacular people in this respect - the workers on the land and such like.

Apart from Ong, two people that I have learned to hold in reverence are George Ewart Evans and Adrian Bell. Whilst some people would describe them as 'foreigners' because they were not locally born, they both took the time to immerse themselves in the people of Suffolk until they understood their mindset. Something that the great folk song collector Alan Lomax said is essential to the study of it (Nash 1991). Neither Bell or Evans endeavoured to write in dialect. Dialect is totally an oral phenomenon, it is not a written phenomenon at all. I believe that it does not translate to hieroglyphical ink stains on a page. Where seen through the eyes of literates practicing 'standard' English it becomes a parody, a Worzelism, almost a Mickey take to those who inherit and naturally use it. I have therefore made no attempt to translate dialect onto these pages. That is left to be interpreted in the readers mind. What is written has to be by its very nature standard English. What is passed orally is our own, our inheritance and our personal identity. Ruby's oral speech, grammar, order of words, sayings and traditional local words I have left in and would not alter them 'for all the tea in china' to use one of her many metaphors.

Ruby was not illiterate, she had been kept on at Sudbury High School until she was 16. She could compose a good business letter and often had to and had a good hand of writing. She had all of the literacy that she needed. Nothing written here has come from the printed source of any prior book, it is all from the true orality, the spoken word of Ruby and just as she told her stories to us as children.

Chapter 1

A fresh young waterlou courted me
he stole my life and sweet liberty
liberty of my own free will
and I must confess, I love him still

There is an Inn in this same town
where my true love goes and sits himself down
he takes another girl on his knee
and tells her things he won't tell me

So it's down in the meadows poor Nellie did go
To gather the flowers as they grow
and every where she gave a pull
until she had gathered here apron full

She gathered the green grass for her bed
a flowery pillow for her head
She laid herself down and no more she spoke
She died poor gal for her heart it was broke

Now love it blows hot, and love it blows cold
It thrills the young and it fills the old
And love it is a terrible thing
It to the grave, poor Nellie did bring

A song learned by Ruby from her mother Emily

My Father was an old bugger that's how he was; he was so hard on me. You know, when I was twelve, during the '14-18 War, we had some wounded soldiers doing convalescent work for us down at Red House Farm. When it came to Christmas time, Father had sold the turkeys to a butcher in Ipswich. When they were to be delivered there was a terrific downpour of snow which made travelling almost impossible. Anyway, the turkeys had to be there or we wouldn't get paid. They were all plucked and ready to be loaded onto the van, but there was nobody to go with them. Neither of the wounded soldiers who we'd got helping us knew the way to Ipswich, which was about 15 miles away, so somebody'd got to go and show them the way. "You've got to go Ruby," said the Old Man. "You can't send that girl", said Mother. He said: "You'll be all right sitting up there next to Charlie Cope. You can wrap yourself in a rug." The snow that kept coming down - that was as cold as charity.

We put Derby, a blue roan mare, in a van, put some straw down at the back, loaded the turkeys and covered them up. It was an open wooden van like a four-wheeled farm cart with iron-tyred wheels and had a board across the front to sit on out in the open. They said: "Well Ruby will have to go, she knows the way there." So I had to go with this man called Charlie Cope, who was a Londoner, to show him the way.

Charlie Cope was a decent sort of chap; he came from Walthamstow and had two sons. His wife was running his little general shop for him while he was in the war. Dad let him go home at weekends and he would bring us back some sugar or the like. He had been wounded in battle at the front, but was getting better. Dad sent him with me because he was more capable than the other one we had. We only had two.

I was well wrapped up and we started off - that was about ten in the morning by the time we got going. When we got as far as Alfred Watson's, the blacksmiths, at Kersey Tye which was just over a mile down the road, we had to stop and have the mare

Dad showing a hackney stallion

shod with spikes, iron spikes screwed into her shoes so she

couldn't slip. The snow kept coming down fast and thick in a blizzard and it was difficult to see. Anyway, the mare still kept slipping about, but we went on to Ipswich and got there. I knew where the place was, so we went down there to the shop and saw the man. We had trouble with him when we got there because he said: "Oh! I don't know. These are not what I expected and the trade's bad and that sort of thing. I think he thought he'd try it on with me as I was not very old. We wanted the money badly, but he said he'd bought them at so much a pound, and that came to so much money, but he was going to knock some off. However, I said that was the price agreed and that was the price it had to be and eventually we got it.

Well, we set sail for home, my fingers and toes were numb they were frawn and when we got as far as Hintlesham George, Charlie Cope said, "I'm gonna get us a drink" and he brought me out a glass of ginger wine to warm me up, and a packet of five Woodbines. I had never smoked before but when he said: "Would you like a smoke?" I said "Yes".

Then we set off from Hintlesham for home, but when we got just outside Hadleigh, where Doctor Taylor was burned at the stake and there's a memorial up there, the mare was more or less taking one step forward and almost one step back, the road was so bad. It was a job for her to get along at all. Then all of a sudden, about a mile out of Hadleigh, she slipped and started to slide at the top of the hill, and her hind legs went from under her. She just sat in her britchins. It was a good job that she had a strong pair of britchins on which held her. She just sat in the britchins and we couldn't stop her, and she kept going, sliding down the hill, from side to side and she slid all the way down the hill right into Hadleigh main street, past the Convent, down Conduit hill, and right into Hadleigh street. When she got into Hadleigh street she managed to stand on her legs again, but all that time she was coming down that hill and she'd lost her legs, and sat in her britchins we couldn't steer her. We hit one side of the road then the other. Luckily we never turned over. No good pulling her left or right, we just couldn't steer her. We never met anything that day but the sky coming down that hill. She just sat and slid, she went top to bottom. Anyway, we got home at about twelve o'clock at night and I went straight away and gave the money to the Old Man. He was in bed asleep.

But even before that time he started to heap responsibility on me. I can't think why or how I stood it. He couldn't seem to take it. I don't know if it's because he never worked as a young man, or that he got bored or something, or if he just couldn't take the bad times. He'd been spoilt and had it easy. Brought up with a silver spoon in his mouth and hadn't had to do nothing. Everyone else had to work hard, but not him, he just took to his bed, sometimes all Winter. He had all his meals served in bed so someone had to keep running upstairs with them. We even had to empty his pot and slop pail, 'cause the only toilet then was outside. I had to go and get the orders for the men. Sometimes they'd all stand beneath the bedroom window and I had to shout the orders out to them from there and keep going back to Dad to hear what he said. Oh, but he'd get up if his friend Stanley Gifford or someone like that was coming, or Charlie Bullock, even then, he just suited himself. He was so selfish. He sponged on everyone in the house. My Mother, Emily, knew what he was like and tried to keep the peace all round, but it was difficult for her. I took most of the brunt of it but no one could do anything right, he was a law unto himself.

Reg Fletcher feeding drum, Ruben Gunn and Goldie Pattle on stack, Betty Kemble next Admiral the greyhound, Edna, Mary Kemble and I, Dad taking corn off drum

If anything went wrong, and it always did, it was always my fault. It was like that when I bought my first horse, Vixen. There was no one going to buy her for me, I was told that if I wanted her I would have to get her myself. Dad lent me the rest of the money and that was almost the only money I got out of him. It was me always lending him after that. Anyhow he made me sweat for it.

Vixen was the name of this horse that I had when I was about 13. Stanley Gifford, Dad's friend owned her. He came over and said "I think I'm going to sell the mare" and he wanted thirteen pounds, ten shillings. Father said "If you want her Ru you'll have to open your money box, you won't get her if you can't raise the wind". She'd been in the army in the 1914-1918 War and had been discharged. She had the 'C' mark branded on her. She had navicular in her feet, but she was as sound as a bell. I opened my moneybox to get my money out. I had ten pounds and I bought Vixen by borrowing the rest from Dad. I was good at

I was only thirteen when I bought Vixen

saving my money. I kept it in a little wooden moneybox with an inlaid marquetry top given to me by my Grand Nan, Nen Pettit. Uncle Steve Alleston had given me a gold sovereign, when he came down from London because his children had been down to stay and I'd looked after them. I'd kept that. I had a five-shilling piece and I had some more money from doing little jobs. The old man said that if I was a good girl and looked after the men when they were thrashing he'd let me off repaying him. He then took to his bed, so I had to go over to The Hollies Farm and sort out how much Tail corn and how much best corn there was and write it all down and take all this information back to him. He wanted to know who was doing what job, who was working on the stack and feeding the drum, and stuff like that. He kept me home from school when this threshing was on. When I was finished he did say "Well done". He was still in bed: "Bring me that IOU", he said, "I'll tear that up" and he did. He really made me work for the money I owed him, and kept me away from school to do it. I was only thirteen. He was pleased then.

Church Street
Boxford
photo courtesy of
Dave Kindred

Chapter 2

There was a frog lived in a mill,
sing song Kitty Kitchi, Ki me oh
If he's not dead he lives there still
sing song Kitty Kitchi, Ki me oh

Dero, diro, dirowar, me I, me o
Me income sally singing sometime periwinkle
Cat nip, cat sing, cat sing song
Kitty Kitchi, Ki me oh.

This was Dad's song, Mother had another version of it that
went:

Frog he would awooing go hey ho said roly
Whether his mother would have let him or no
With a roly poly gammon and spinach hey ho said antony roly

I didn't like that old song though because the last verse was:

A lily white duck came and gobble him up…
With a roly poly gammon and spinach hey ho said anthony roly

To start at the beginning. I was born at River House, Bures on the 27th December 1905, the day after Boxing Day and Christened Ruby Jesse Alleston. Then there was little Dick who died. He was born on 21st May 1907. Then Edna, 9th June 1910, Claude, 27th August 1912 and last of all, fourteen years later on, was Tickles. He was christened Hugh Charles after his Uncle, but he was so ticklish as a little baby that he got that nickname and it stuck with him for the rest of his life.

Dad had come from Bures and my mother Emily from Stratford St Mary. I think that Dad was like he was because he was the only son, and his parents, old Charlie and Martha had been so poor to start with, coming from such poor homes. They had worked so extremely hard to get a few bob, that when they had some, they gave him whatever he wanted. They did have a difficult time in those old days, I'll tell you as far back as I was told.

Myslelf aged one year

River House Bures where I was born on 27th December 1905

My Grandfather and my Grandmother, on Dad's side, were very poor people. Grandmother was born somewhere between Melford and Rodbridge in one of those little flint houses along the main road, just before you get to where the old toll gate used to be, but that's all gone now. Their name was Bonny. Father's mother was Martha Bonny, she was one of several children, mostly girls. I don't know what her father did for a living, but he had a job to make enough for the family. He used to make whitening balls at night time with chalk, and he'd go around selling 'em, 'three balls a penny'. They called him 'old three balls a penny' because that's what he shouted out. He was a poor old boy. Eventually Martha left home - she packed up and went up to London. Before that she was a silk weaver in Sudbury. Vanners, I think the name of the company

16

was, she was a silk weaver and so was her sister. Her sister, my Aunt Sarah, married Tom Clark from Bures. Boating was very popular then, so they made a bit of money at it. They built a boathouse at Bures and they used to hire boats out. They also used to make ginger beer and old Tom Clark, in his horse and cart, used to go round and sell it to the pubs. Martha Bonny met my Grandfather, old Charlie Alleston, before she went to London.

Granddad Alleston was one of a family of twelve and worked in the Tanyard at Bures. The family of Allestons all worked in the Tanyard - his father and all the boys as well. I heard say, they used to bring home 'Tanyard meat' which is the meat from the lips of the bullock and places like that, that isn't worth going to the butchers and they used to skin the lip off boil that up and the meat from the head. Not all the bits from the head, only if it was good meat and the scraping off the skins and that like. They used to tan the hides, shake the hides out and all that.

Granddad Alleston went to London first, then Grandma followed him up. She went to London in service in some big house, she was paid twelve pounds ten shillings a year and her keep. She didn't get as much as that though when she first started. When she became the cook she had some perks, like from the butcher who used to deliver the meat for the big house, he used to give her a Christmas box. She also used to boil all the

Myself at River House

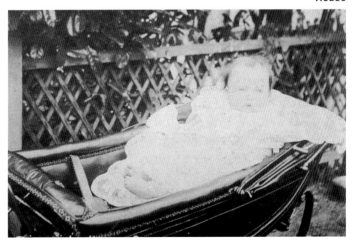

fat down to make packets of it, which she used to sell as dripping. Poor people lived on bread and dripping, if not they had to have bread and pull-it, bread and pull-it boy what do you think of that?

When Granddad decided he was going to London, he got a better job up there, because he was a horse-man and he went in charge of a yard of brewers' horses. Charringtons the brewers were. He had twenty-four horses to look after, he used to get some perks as well. If a horse was queer he knew in a minute and he knew what to do. The vet said he could give a horse a ball or a drench and things like that if he thought it needed it, so he saved the vet a lot of running backwards and forwards and at the end of the year the vet would give Granddad a sweetener.

When he was in digs in London the great thing he missed was his feather bed. He wrote home and asked them to send him a feather bed up from Bures. Granddad's nick-name was 'Tights' for some reason, Charlie Tights they called him. Perhaps that's because was careful with his money. One day the LNER van called and they said "We've a parcel here for Charlie Alleston," they went to the door and the Landlady said "I'm sorry I haven't got anyone of that name here." She said "The only person I've got here is Charlie Tights." After a day or two Granddad said, "I don't understand, I sent for that feather bed by rail, it ought to have been here before now, I can't work it out." She said: "What did you say it was?" He said: "It was a feather bed, it should have been here ages ago." "Well." she said, "A man from the railway called the other day and they had a parcel on board for Charlie Alleston but you're Charlie Tights. So Grandfather didn't get his feather bed.

Grandma saved her money and he saved his and when they got enough money together they got married. Granddad got a job working evenings in charge of a beer garden. My Father said that if people didn't finish their beer, he used to put it in a bucket and when someone ordered beer next, they'd get one out of there and he'd pocket the money. I'm not sure if that's true, but he certainly was careful. They saved up all the money they could. They really scraped round for it. Then a pub came up to let in a rough quarter, but they took it. That was called The Cooper's Arms. That was in Union Street, Borough, the borough of Southwark right in the heart of London within the sound of Bow Bells, so they moved into that. Before they moved in there, they had two children, one was Jessie Alleston, and one was Charlie Alleston - young Charles my father. You see, there were

The Coopers Arms Union Street Borough. My Grandfather Chas. Alleston in front with sleeves rolled. He often had to get over the counter to sort out trouble and slept with a sword under his bed

two Charlie's, 'Old', my grandfather and 'Young', my Father, I'll just call the young one, my Dad 'the old man' or Charles and his father old Charlie, so you don't get confused.

Charles Alleston 'the old man' was not born at the time that his sister died, she was about two when Grandma was expecting again. Jessie died of whooping cough about three months before Charles was born which was about the time that they moved into The Cooper's Arms. Granddad took it on a thirteen-year lease, and they were there nine years when they made enough money to buy a house down in Bures. They bought a house, a horse and cart and they retired and lived in Bures. When they retired they had some people called Salter to manage the pub for them to the end of the lease. These people, Salter, that went in, were Uncle Steve's wife's brother and his wife. Anyway Granddad had made enough money to buy a house in the country, he had a bob or two

and he was comfortable. But he put these beggars in to manage the pub for him and they put him in debt in the first year. Instead of making money they hadn't made any money - they were robbing him right, left and centre, hand over fist. He put them in there to manage the pub, that he had been making a good profit out of and they robbed him blind. He wasn't going to be robbed by them anymore, so what did he do? He shut his house up in the country and went back to London, and back in the pub to finish the lease out.

They had to work damned hard in that pub. That was the time of day when you could go in there and you could get five things for a penny. If you bought a tot of rum, that was a penny, with it you could have a pinch of snuff, a pinch of tobacco, a look at the Sporting Life and something else, five things all for a penny.

On bank holidays and Sundays, they say that Old Charlie used to brew up himself. He had to do it on those days, because weekdays the Excise man kept popping round. Anyway he saved £20,000 in the twenty years he was in London, which was a small fortune in those days. But that was hard work and he always slept with a sword under his bed, in case they had an intruder. He often had to leap over the counter to sort someone out. He could handle his fists.

Dad was not brought up in this pub in London. They would not have him in that rough place, so they sent him back to Suffolk. He was brought up in Bures by his Aunt Sarah the wife of Tom Clark, the ginger beer man. He went to Sudbury Grammar School and travelled on his a pony, six miles there and six miles back every day. During the day he used to keep it at The Christopher, an old pub in Gainsborough Street.

Buffalo Bill came over with his wild west troupe and he went into their pub. They had a signed picture of him on the wall then.

Dad whilst at St Olaves Grammar School London

Grandmother's sister, Aunt Sarah, and Tom Clark looked after Charles. They had several children. They had young Tom and another boy, then there was Maud Clark who married a Mussett, and there was Isobel who was never a very strong person. Charles lived there with them and Aunt Sarah thought a rare lot of him. She used to sit next to him, and if there was anything left over, a little bit of pudding or something like that, she always used to ask Charles first, and their own children used to get a bit jealous. By this time my father was getting on. He was about eighteen. He went back up to town because they wanted him to start work. They wanted him to go to Hatton Garden to be a diamond merchant. That's what Granddad wanted him to be and some people who used to use the public house got him in. Granddad bought him his diamond cutter's apron and tools all ready, but he went once and said: "Oh. I don't like that old job I ain't going no more." and he never went no more. Then Granddad finally retired from the pub and came back down to Suffolk and Dad came back down here with his father.

When Dad came to River House, Bures, he was about eighteen or nineteen. He was not tall, but he was a handsome young man with black hair and was always liked by the ladies wherever he went. He had a taste for good clothes and with his father's money, was immaculate. He'd got away with everything. If he didn't want to work, like in Hatton Garden or anywhere else, then he didn't have to. In fact, he didn't do anything until he was twenty-two years old. He spent some of this time in London. He had a friend up there and they used to go round the Music Halls together, and that's how he knew all those songs.

When Dad came down to Suffolk he met Stanley Gifford. Stanley was a daredevil and would do anything for a wager. Charles soon got in with the social set around Bures, and he met my Grandmother. She was step-daughter to the Warrens, who had a big circle of friends such as the Giffords.

Stanley Gifford Dad's daredevil friend

and Dad (right)

Chapter 3

With a rip-a-tip a turn him out
And a hunting let him go
For many long miles they hunted me
In the woods for many long day
Poor old horse, poor old horse

Me skin I'll give to the huntsman
And me body to the hounds
No more will I be talked about
All on the Hunting grounds
Poor old horse, poor old horse

When I was young and in me prime
And in me stable lay
I used to be fed on the very best corn
Like will the very best hay
Poor old horse, poor old horse

But now I'm old and past me prime
And fit for nothing at all
I have to eat the sour grass
That grows along the wall
Poor old horse, poor old horse

One of Dad's songs

When Dad was about twenty, he went to Colchester shopping one day with his father, old Charlie. Dad always used to bring some haddock home and they would put it in a fish basket. Granddad had been to buy some haddock, and my father was standing on the pavement when a chap came up to him and accused him of something he wasn't guilty of and called him names and was swearing at him. This chap was standing in the road and starting to throw his fists. My father did not want to make a scene in Colchester High Street, but a crowd started to gather and while he stood there along came Grandfather with these haddocks in a fish basket. He walked up to my Father and said: "What's happening? What's all this about? What's he shouting about?" Dad said: "Oh, he wants to fight" so Grandfather made no more ado about it at all, he just said: "Hold my haddocks boy" and put the haddock in Dad's hand. He stepped off the pavement, drew him off a couple and laid him out. He wasn't young then and this chap was a big feller, but Granddad had been used to it in that rough old pub. After that if anything needed dire attention we'd say 'Hold my Haddocks'.

I've heard Grandma tell the story about when they were at the pub how Granddad often had to get over the counter to put somebody out. Once a chap was being a nuisance in the pub, so he put him outside and when he got him outside, this chap was saucy to Granddad and Granddad didn't make any bones, he just smacked him one - drew him off one and knocked him down. I think the police come along. Granddad had knocked this bloke down you see and his pals stood by him and Granddad had to go to court. One of Grandma's brothers was employed up there as potman in the pub and he had to go as a witness. When he got in the witness box, he was supposed to be on Granddad's side of course, but he got in the there, the fool, he said: "Yes, Charlie drew him off one and knocked him out" So Granddad had to pay, cause you see he'd said the wrong thing.

Grandma Alleston, Martha, she hadn't got a corn, she had perfect feet and she had skin like a lily. She was a very perky old girl, she always wore a full black cloth skirt, right down to the ground. She wore button sided boots and she would wear black corsets that laced up. She had a high collar with a bit of lace around the top and when she was a little bit fed up or she heard someone saying anything she didn't like, she'd say "Oh dear, well there it is, every generation grows weaker and wiser and the weakest must go by the wall".

The toilet was outside and Grandma was over eighty. You had to go round with a candle and there were rats in the bottom of the toilet. You see it was cleaned out only about once every six months. The soil cart used to come and clean it out. Anyway, there was a rat down the bottom there and it had to come up into the toilet you see, so my father said "I'll set a trap in there for that, I'll stop his laughing in church". So he set a trap and he went to Grandma, got hold of her and said: "I want to show you something. Now you see that in there, don't you. I've set a trap there for a rat, so what ever you do, don't put your hand down against that will you? That's a rat trap and that will break your hand" After a couple of hours she came in with it on her hand. I took it off her and bathed her hand. She just couldn't keep out of anything, she just had to interfere.

My old man, he went to bed in the winter-time, and wouldn't get up. He used to keep me on the go, going backwards and forwards across to the Hollies Farm. I had to look for this and look for that; he nearly drove me shanny. I remember a cow calving, the after birth was left back and it was hanging out. Harry kept saying to me "You ought to have the vet to that cow" but we'd got a dog tied up at the vets , we hadn't paid him. I said: "Dad, that cow needs attention. If not that will go bad. He said: "If anything happens to that cow it's your fault", that's what he said to me. "You're in charge of looking after those cows over there, and if anything happens to her, it's your fault", I said: "Well if you don't let the vet come, I'll get the vet to come 'cause I'm sure something will happen to her", I got so worried with all the responsibility. Getting rid of the afterbirth though is not so important as it is with a horse. If anything is left behind after a foal, that can go bad and the poison will go to their feet and give them laminitus.

*Mother's father
Arthur Dean Pettit*

Mother's maiden name was Petitt - Emily Pettit and she lived at Bures Hall with her stepfather, Old Warren or Fob as we called him. You see Mother's mother had married again. I remember my Mother telling me about her family. There were two brothers and their father and mother died when they were quite young, but they were left Fordham Hall, Nr Colchester. Their name was Pettit. Their parents must have been comfortably off, and the two boys were left everything. They even had their own silver and it had the Pettit stamp on it and a nice lot of jewellery. I don't know who it was, but somebody went into the farm to look after it until these boys were old enough to farm it, when they were 21. Somewhere along the line one brother died, I don't know what his name was, but that left Arthur Dean Pettit, who was my Mother's father. When he was old enough to take over his money, the people who had brought him up at Fordham Hall took a certain amount of the money because they said it cost that much to bring him up. A lot of money they charged, about six thousand. Then Arthur Dean married and he married his cousin, she was also a Pettit, Kate Pettit. She lived at Mount Bures. They were a big family and Kate was the youngest. They were only married eight years when he died and she was left with two sons and a daughter, Hugh, George and my mother, Emily, the youngest one. Grandmother, Kate Pettit (Nen we called her) had not been a widow long when she was introduced to old Mr Warren. He was an undertaker and his wife had hanged herself, so he was a widower with one son. He knew Kate Pettit was a widow, and she'd got a farm and he thought she was very desirable, so Mr Warren got a Mr Knott, who was a cousin of Kate's to introduce him. They used to throw a lot of parties that time of day - usually card parties - and Mr Warren got Knott to have a party and invite Grandma Pettit there. Kate Pettit duly arrived at the party that night and of course old Warren was there and he got friendly with her and that sort of thing. It was not long before he proposed marriage, he was accepted, and of course he moved in with Grandma Pettit. I don't know how well off he was then, but Grandmother had a nice bit of money when they married. Mr Warren hadn't got any money. He had one son called Roly, who went to fight in the Boer War. Mr Warren took over and relieved Grandma of the running of the farm, and even took over her bank account. They lived at Bures Hall, then they went to Stratford Hall at Stratford St Mary, and then onto Peyton Hall, Boxford. My mother was married from Stratford Hall, that's where she was living with her two brothers when she married.

Her brothers, Hugh and George, were no good and wouldn't work. George went to Canada and while they were at Bures Hall Hugh married Kate, his cousin. She was

Mother's brother George Pettit who emigrated to Canada

Deborah's daughter and Mr Warren put them in a little farm, just outside Bures somewhere. He started them off, not a very big farm but a little farm that he could run on his own, but Hugh was always down the pub. Hugh went through his money, so he took a job and he went to work for a man, he worked for that man until the day he died. He must have done something to have stayed in the job but Dad was always running him down. When they came over to see Mother, Dad used to criticise and pooh pooh them. Hugh would drink and eat all he could and the old man made up a song about him: 'There came a man from the Essex shore who had three helpings and wanted more ...' it went. Hugh and Kate had six children and all of 'em did well. Aubrey Pettit the eldest one is a builder at Risley, then Stan and the youngest one, Peter, but he was more trouble than any of them, he was more like his father. I think he was a hairdresser or something, but one of the boys is a landscape gardener, and is comfortably off, I believe.

Old Fob Warren used to sing a song that went:

> I love me wife, me pipe and me glass
> Merrily along life's road I do pass
> Jolly and free and that just suits me
> And I'm off with me gun in the morning

They all used to sing that time of day. Every one had a party piece - you had to when you were out in company, you couldn't let the side down. 'Never have it said boy, yer Mother bred a jibber,' they'd say, so you had to play your part.

When Mr Warren married my Grandmother, they had two more children, Philip and Charlie. When she was a young girl, Mother used to look after those boys. They moved to Peyton Hall at Boxford. When I was very young we would all go over there for Christmas. Charlie was older than me, and I can remember them saying: "Whatever you do, don't go anywhere near that gobbler," you know, a turkey cock, "If you see him anywhere come right back in the house." They could knock you down and peck your eyes out, they were horrible. If you got a bad'un and he was a real bad'un, to a little child they could be dangerous. I remember the lawn, a lovely lawn outside, but one day that blinking old gobbler got out round there and he came running after me, that old gobbler, I ran back into the house, I could not have been more than three or four.

After Peyton Hall, Boxford the Warrens moved to Graves Hall, Sible Hedingham, where they stayed. When they were at Graves Hall and Charlie Warren was about twelve, just a bit older than me we were up there spending Christmas and they were expecting Roly Warren to come. That was Grandfather Warren's stepson. He was married to a very smart young lady, she was a real good looker like a film star. She was manageress of The Cups at Colchester, she was not a barmaid, she was the manageress. I can remember Roly and his wife driving up in a cart pulled by a dun pony. There was a long sweeping drive, we were looking out of a window upstairs, Charlie and I. He said: "Come on Ruby look out of the window and say, hello Roly, how's your Mrs?, my Mother was ever so cross.

At Graves Hall, they used to play a lot of croquet on the lawn in the Summer and there used to be a little sweet shop down the road. When Roly came back from the Boer War he got married and old Mr Warren gave him a farm. He put him in Houchins Farm, Bures. He set him up in business with his own farm. Old

My mother Emily

Mr Warren had got a set of black Worcesters and I have heard my Mother say all the rows that were caused in that family were through those two boys, her brothers. Old Mr Warren was good to my Mother though, he bought her a new bicycle, when bicycles were at a premium. They kept cows and they had a big dairy. People in those days used to come to the door for milk. They used to serve out pints of milk and the money was always put in a drawer and Grandma used it as part of her housekeeping money, but Mother's brothers used to nick it, they'd pinch it. I heard Mother say that when she went to the drawer, there would be no money in there because they had taken it. Then of course, old Mr Warren used to kick up a row. That was quite right really.

Roly Warren had one son, Ford, and they eventually farmed Fordham Hall, where Grandfather Pettit was brought up. Ford went to Colchester Grammar School and when he left school, he went to London. He went to Covent Garden as a salesman, to learn the business up there. They reckoned Roly would buy a field of turnips and send them up there and Ford would sell them in Covent Garden, but the 1914-1918 War came. Roly quickly put Ford to work on a farm to save him going to the front. Sprots Farm at Polstead was what he bought for him. If you were coming from Polstead home to Boxford, round that bad corner and up, then you'd turn left to go to Boxford, but if you take the other road straight on, there's a farm down there on the right, Sprots farm - a bad old farm. Later they sold it and Ford eventually went to a farm just the other side of Colchester, on the London Road.

Philip Warren, would play snooker then for £25 a time, he'd play anyone and Charlie, his brother, won loads at cards. They would go to Newmarket Races and on the way and coming home always stopped at The Rose & Crown at Gt Thurlow where they would play cards and bet all night. People would come from miles around in the pony traps to join in, even their local doctor would hire a pony and trap special for it. Charlie won a mushroom farm one night in there at cards. Both those boys married daughters of publicans. Aunty Beatie, Philip's wife, was the only girl and she came from somewhere near Sible Hedingham. Charlie's wife, Kate, was a Tillbrook and came from The Queens Head at Thurlow. It was where the garage stands now. She was a wonderful cook and a lot of mum's pudding recipes came from her. When I went up there as a little girl at Christmas one year, it always impressed me when you opened the doors at Graves Hall there was everything you could think of. All the old antique things, there was a great big antlers head that came nearly across the hall, from one side to the other. There was the breakfast room and the music room, just as you got in the door. Further down the hall was the drawing room where they had some most exquisite china. I can remember that china and mother used to say "Mind you don't break anything." There was a great big staircase and landing as well, and a large old kitchen and a dining room. They had some little things, they were more like pegs dressed up, they were on strings and I remember sitting on one side of the hearth and holding the string with Mr Warren sitting on the other side of the hearth and a great big roaring fire and I can remember them dancing like puppets. Another thing they had was a roundabout, I don't know what there was in the middle, but you used to wind it up and the roundabout went round, there were horses like the gallopers used to be. It was made of tin.

Kare Warren's recipe that mum always used. She always wrote down the name of everybody she got her recipes from, then she knew how good they were - Kate Warren's were the best

My Father did not get on very well with Mr Warren though, because my Dad got my Mother into trouble before they were married and old Warren made sure he didn't run off, which I think he might have done. Dad used to drive a smashing little trotting pony, he was dressed smart, spoke well and always welcome at the house. Grandma Kate thought the world of him and she encouraged him there and he used to see my Mother, but he took my Mother out just once too often, and that was that. That annoyed old Warren, he was a straight man and he wouldn't put up with no pielaw from Dad. They were married on 13th September 1905 and I was born at Christmas. Old Fob Warren, Mother's father, gave them £100, that was her dowry. She didn't have anything other than that and my Father always thought my Mother ought to have had more out of her Father's estate. He did give her £100, but the cheque was post dated, so they couldn't have been too well off. My Father, not Mr

Christmas Puddings

12 oz Bread Crumbs
2 lbs Flour.
2 lbs Suet.   (1½ Suet)
2 tea spoons Salt.
1 lb Moist Sugar.   (1½ Sugar)
2 lbs Stoned Raisens.
1/2 lb Currants.
2 oz mixed Peel, Citron, Almonds & Prunes.
1 lb Apples.
5 Eggs. etc.
1/2 pt of Sherry, Brandy & milk
Boil for 9 hours.
                              K. Warren.

Warren, kept my Mother away from them, she would have spent a lot more time with her own mother if it hadn't of been for the fact that my father would say: "Oh you don't want to go to those beggars" and decrying them, that sort of thing. Father never encouraged their friendship and that was only because he was sore. Sore because he thought that my Mother ought to have had more money, and that Old Warren had been mean. In the dining room at Graves Hall was a beautiful picture of a horse standing in the stable, looking in the manger, Hugh had it. After he'd gone away and got married he kept saying it was his Father's picture and he ought to have it. When Mr Warren died Philip wanted to be fair so he said: "Well Hugh always said that was his picture" so Philip put it in his car and took it down to Hugh and the last I heard of it Aubrey had it, the eldest boy.

When Mother lived at Stratford Hall, Stanley Gifford's family lived along side the river. My mother was courting Dad then. Stanley was about her age and he never cared a bugger about anybody. The Giffords were aristocrats and were well off then going down there was like going into the land of Goshen. They used to have the barges on the river and when they gave a party they'd have two or three barges tied together and they'd have a piano on one barge and they'd go up and down the river at Stratford and Dedham. Stanley used to sing. They used to have a right old do. Mother used to be invited to their parties, she was single and my Father used to be a bit jealous. Mother also used to go to parties at Thorington House, Thorington Street, Stoke by Nayland. When they had a do at Christmas and you were invited to a party you stopped there all night, because it was a long way to drive home in a horse and trap.

Where the tow paths came to an end the horse was trained to step onto a flat board on the front of the barge and the bargeman would then drift over to the other bank and the horse would automatically get off. Oil painting belonging to Ruby by P F Hitchcock Flatford

The barges on the River Stour were pulled two at a time by a horse along a towpath. The towpath changed banks so many times that to get these horses over the river they trained them so that they would jump onto the flat piece at the front of the barge when the two path ended. The man in the barge would then steer it over to the other side of the river where the horse would jump off and start pulling the barge again along the new tow path. They had no rudders. The man sat at the back of the barge and had a long tiller onto the rear barge that steered it. The Giffords had lots of barges and would collect corn for their mill as far up the river as Sudbury and beyond in the olden days.

Dad was a long time before he started work so he must have had a long time messing about. Stanley Gifford became his best friend and they got up to all sorts of high jinks. They used to get in The Rose at Thorington Street and they'd ride to some barn doors over the fields and take anyone on and that included jumping a five-bar gate on the way. That was all for wagers, for money. Stanley got reduced in circumstances and ended up renting a little cottage by the river down at Gt Henny and he earned a living just poaching or he'd break a horse for someone that no one else could break and he trained greyhounds. He was a terrific sport, he was an athlete and would take anyone on at anything. I remember him taking his pony and trap over to an athletics meeting at Lavenham and winning lots of silver but on his way back home he lost it all. He got drunk and turned the cart over and Dad went to help him find it the next morning, but all they found were a few spoons. His old pony died, so Dad would give him a young horse to break in, then he'd have that back and give him another one, and Dad would always send the feed over with it. Once when he was poaching up the river at Henny he shot a pheasant, he put his son and the dog on shore to get it. Someone

Stratford Hall, Stratford St Mary where Emily Petit, my mother lived before she married

caught to boy, so Stanley picked the dog up and brought it back. Of course he had to go to court, as they had caught his boy so they knew it was him. In court he made them laugh. When they asked him why he only picked the dog up he said "The dog was worth more money." That dog's name was Jim and he left the dog outside a pub once, in charge of game - to sit there and guard it. He thought the world of that dog and someone went up and interfered with it. Stanley went out of that pub and gave him such a hiding. He wouldn't stand no truck would Stanley.

Once when he was out he went into a shop in Debenham, Abbots that was called, (I think it's still there now) and saw a young lady in there. He went outside and said to the old man: "I'm going to marry that girl" and he did. Her father didn't approve and they had to pass notes out of the window at night-time and all that sort of thing. Then she ran away and married him.

He'd eat steak raw you know. One time when he had been in jail for poaching, Dad picked him up and took him into to bar in Sudbury. Dad got him some steak and as he ate it he spat a bit of gristle out on the bar floor, someone complained so he put it back in his mouth and swallowed it, - just to show 'em - that's how he was. When he'd come over to see Grandfather sometimes he'd sleep rough on the way, he didn't care. Stanley would sing and he would dress up and sing at concerts, and his wife would play the piano for him. Everyone loved him.

When he was with Dad one day in a pub in Sudbury, there was

Dad

some athlete in there boasting what a wonderful swimmer he was. Old Stanley couldn't put up with that any longer so he said: "I'll take you on". This fellow said, "Yes Where and when then?" So Stanley said: "Here, Ballingdon Bridge to Henny Swan, fully clothed, middle of Winter". They all had bets - wagers on it, between them and Dad put up several sovereigns on Stanley's side. The day came round - I think that was Boxing day - Stanley turned up just as he was and just took off his jacket and boots. This fellow was all in light flannels and thin shirt. Away they went, straight in. Of course Stanley soon left him, he was at Henny Swan drying himself in front of the open fire there when this fellow was still clambering up the bank. Dad said: "I've got some dry clothes for you to put on Stanley". "That's all right Charles," he said: "I'll just stand here in front of this fire, I'll be dry in a few minutes". The room was filled with steam coming off Stanley's clothes. Dad said: "Shall I get the Landlady to cook this steak for you?" Stanley said: "No, no, give it here boy, I'll have it as it is". He didn't change or nothing, and never moved from that spot in front of the fire.

Otters were plentiful then and there were a lot up and down the river. They were a pest and eating the fish. Normally you wouldn't kill an otter because the otter hounds used to hunt them, but during the years of the 1914-1918 War the otter hounds didn't come round and there got so many of them that Stanley used to trap them on the river and he would send the Pelts to London. He said he'd get me one which he did. It was three quarters grown and measured three foot six from the tip of its nose to the sole of it's feet. He sent it to London and had it specially cured right for me and I sent it back up there again and had it made into a fur stole. He used to sell these otter skins. You could make a lot of money of an otter skin that time of the day. He'd have traps laid all up the River Stour at Henny, where he lived. One day he came over and put two live otters in our big water butt, they couldn't get out. Then, the next day he took them up to Sudbury, Market Hill, where he charged six pence a look for the hospital funds. When a woman complained she couldn't see the otters in the cage, he thrust his hand in, pulled one out and put it on her lap. She never asked no more. Poor old Stanley died in 1926. It was an accident. His horse and trap stopped suddenly. He was thrown forward and the shaft of the cart ran through him. Dad was very upset. He lost his best friend. There's always that danger with a horse and trap.

Chapter 4

Jerusal-i-em Cuckoo

I am an old donkey driver the best in all the line
There's not another dickey that can come up to mine
You can talk about Jerusalem and other donkeys too
There's not a donkey on the line can beat Jerusalem Cuckoo

CH
Shout boys hurrah, trouble I have few
Not a donkey on the line can beat Jerusalem Cuckoo
I took the old donkey to Epsom, I backed him in a race
And thinking my old donkey would run a tender pace
But when the command was given the donkey nearly flew
For a rattling of a race was Jerusalem Cuckoo

CH
I took the old donkey to Brighton all on the Brighton sands
A lady jumped onto his back and passed the German bands
The donkey turned a dancing and away the lady flew
For a rattling and a dancing was Jerusalem Cuckoo

CH
I managed to get a bit of meat, my donkey he gets hay
And if the old mo kicks the bucket I know what I would do
I would lay me down and die the side of my Jerusalem Cuckoo.

I learned this from Harry Tricker I think or one of the
other men on the farm, they would sing all day.

In 1900 when my Father was 22, his Father started him in
business - he never did anything at all until he was 22. His Father
had money from keeping the pub in London and Dad was his
only son and he had everything he wanted. He'd just done
nothing 'til then, just messed around, so Grandfather put him in
business in the hay trade in Bures. Dad bought two beautiful

new horse-drawn vans, which he had made in London regardless of the expense, and he had them 'till the day he died. One of them was a van with sides and the other one was a van with just the front, a trolley like the old railway ones used to be - nothing at the side just a seat at the front. He had all the best harness made and all the brass plates had his initials engraved on and right big pads. Darkie Spooner worked for him then in the hay and coal trade. I don't know if he did much in coal, but what he used to do was contract to the Garrison in Colchester by guaranteeing so many tons of hay and straw and the like. He bought two or three hay presses and the men worked them in gangs and stacked it for so much a ton. He did that until 1902 or a little longer.

The old man had a lovely little pony then called Roxanne that could trot. She was a trotting pony and only stood 11.2h. When

Lavenham Horse Fair. It never got going again after the 14-18 war there just weren't enough horses

you looked over the side of the cart when it was trotting you couldn't see its legs move, they went so fast. He bought it off some travelling people at Lavenham horse fair before the 14-18 war. The people that had that pony took it to this fair pulling a sort of orange box on wheels. Dad made up his mind to buy it and buy it he did. They said that they didn't want to sell it but he hung about and kept offering more until he got it. When he got it home he had a trotting dilly, a Sulky specially made for it in London. They sent her measurements up there and this lightweight cart with big wheels made for just one person came back. She went like the wind. It was like owning a racing car in those days. Automobiles were just getting about then and Stanley Gifford would race them riding along the verge on his mare Vixen. He had been beaten by this man Fred Kingsbury from Boxford. Trotting ponies were prized possessions and legendary in their races and Dad had seen a print of one. One day coming back from Hadleigh market the old man took on Fred Kingsbury and his automobile for a wager. Roxanne won covering the five miles from Hadleigh market to Boxford Swan in 11 minutes. Mr Chambers at Bures who was a Jobmaster kept plaguing my father to sell it to him. One day, I don't know if he

Young Stanley Ribbons, Scarfe the Miller, Ribbons Butcher, Gardener - the Papershop, George Gooden - pub landlord, Roxanne with Dad - Charles Alleston in the trotting dilly

was hard up or what, but he sold it to Mr Chambers. When that walked into Chambers yard, he said "There you are Charlie, that will never come out this yard no more. That will never come out of here to belong to anybody else. That's mine and I'm keeping it." He swore he'd never sell it.

My Father used to take me out when he was driving the gig to go and buy hay. I wasn't old enough to sit on the seat in case I fell off, I used to stand between his legs in the front. I remember going though Gazely Gate, at Assington, it is near Aga Fen woods. It's all little fir trees and masses and masses of bluebells. The whole place is blue. It's ever so pretty, there's a little stream at the bottom of the hill, then you go up the other hill. When you get on the top, there's a wood on the left and you can look back on it and it is so beautiful. We used to go up the top, when he was going to Mr Emery's farm which was called Smallbridge Hall. When we would get there he'd leave the horse and gig and would go and look at some hay. Smallbridge Farm had a moat all round it and a drawbridge. It was just like olden times round there. It was beautiful. Dad used to buy up the hay, and send it up to the Garrison. Mr Emery and his wife gave Mum and Dad a wedding present, the barometer that still hangs in the hall at the Red House. Dad would tap it as he passed night and morning, to see which way the weather was moving. In my courting days we often went to Gazely Gate and we used to take picnics down there with the whole family. Some years later I said that I would go over and look at the bluebells with Ted Tritton on his motor bike. He was going to take me on his great big old motor bike that was built for Tom Skinner by Triumphs. Tom Skinner was a haulage contractor and lived at Baker Street Green, he weighed over twenty stone. I cycled down to the village to meet Ted. When I got down there he had broken his wrist, so he couldn't ride the motor bike. So I rode that great old motor bike over there and Ted sat on the back. I've been down there with the hounds as well. We would go down the hill to the stream, then up the other side to the wood called Aga Fen. There was always a fox in there.

Another pretty place that I used to go was Homey Bridge. It's down behind Polstead Park and along some meadows and

Charles, Dick, Ruby, Emily and Edna

watercress used to grow there, beautiful. I used to get over a stile I don't know whose meadow it was, but I used to pick this watercress and I used to take a fish basket, an old fashioned woven fish basket and fill it right brim full. Then they cleaned out the stream and it didn't grow no more so I used to go to Assington. When you get to Assington where you turn right to go towards Bures, I used to go straight over and down a stream and there was a farm there that Muriel Rainsford and her sister had. In the river down there was miles of watercress. Freshly gathered Watercress. In sandwiches of new bread and butter you cannot beat.

In 1902, my Granddad, Old Charlie, bought Red House Farm. That was then in the parish of Boxford. It cost £12.00 an acre and there was 160 acres. I think it was his idea to breed horses as they were always his great love. Granddad came to live at Red House Farm and left Dad River House, Bures to live in. Dad was still doing his Garrison contract, but he packed that in after a while and went just into farming. Granddad bought those cottages up

Red House Farm Boxford, Suffolk. Bought in 1905 for twelve pounds an acre

the road from the Red House Farm towards Boxford. They were called 'The Oblong', and he moved there, and eventually let Dad live in the farmhouse.

Then in 1908 when I was three and a half years old, he bought Sampsons Hall, Kersey, which is about a mile and a half nearer to Kersey village, but on the same road. It's about a mile out of Kersey. My sister Edna, was born in the June of 1910 and in the September we moved down there to Sampsons Hall. Mrs Sycamore, I remember, was the woman who used to nurse Mother and she came from Bures. She used to live in the next door house to Tom Clark, so that's how we knew her. She was a midwife. Mother had her second child fairly quick, she didn't want that second child as quick as that. She'd got one. She didn't want the second one so the old lady gave her some stuff called Penny Royal, whatever that is. Mother took this Penny Royal, but she didn't have a miscarriage, she still carried the child and Mother always used to think that had some effect on the child taking that stuff. It was a crime then but there was nothing else you could do. Anyway, Dick was born on 21st May 1907. When he was quite young he fell off a window ledge and hit his head. That poor boy was taken to Colchester Hospital where they said he had a clot of blood on the brain and they couldn't do anything for him. He died when he was six and is buried in Kersey Churchyard opposite the door, alongside the path where you go into the Church. He did not have a tombstone.

Edna was the next child, she was born on 9th June 1910. I can remember quite well the day we all moved to Sampsons Hall. They took Edna in the pram and I walked down the side of the pram to Kersey. It was a long way to walk. The old

Dick Alleston aged one and a half years on his favourite mare bonnie black bess

Penn, our mothers help, Edna on donkey, mother and myself

man never said much at all to me. Anyway we all went down there and the first year we were there he bought two mares together, Derby and Smart. They had a lovely orchard down there, and Blossom was the first foal of this mare called Derby, who was a blue roan mare, and Bumper was her father. He was a little Shire stallion and he wasn't very big and we called him Bumper, 'cause Dad bought him at Mr Kemballs sale and Mr Kemball's nick-name was Bumper. When that foal was born it had a blaze down its face. It was a lovely foal and so quiet, you could do anything with it. They put me on this little foal's back and that never used to jump about, it was so kind and that used to suck its mother and I'd be on its back. We had her for years and she was the only mare we had that could move a drum was Blossom. We usually had to put two or three horses on to move it, but if there were times they could not move it we would put Blossom on and she would stand on her hind legs to move it off on her own. She would rear up to get a start! We had a donkey when we were down there, Granddad bought a donkey.

We had a mother' help then called Penn. Pleasance Rosa Middleton her name was, and she used to walk with us down Kersey village. I think that father was involved with her but I did not know till later. There was a snob there, a bootmaker and repairer in the village, and I could just get my nose above his half door. He'd be cobbling all day long. When I went there he always gave me some money and I used to buy sherbet. At Boxford there was a farmer and dealer called Walter Ribbons and he used to give me sixpence sometimes as well. That was a lot of money in those days. I've known him go past to Kersey in his horse and cart and stop and leave sixpence for me. He was always very fond of me as a little girl. He had some children of his own, but they were all younger than me. He lived in Swan Street.

Fetler King and Bumper the small stallion bought at Kemballs sale in 1901

One day we went blackberrying down to the meadows and the sun was so strong, it was so hot. I was with Penn. I was 6 or 7. I got sunstroke badly because I didn't have a hat on, I was delirious and I could see things going up the wall and I was shaking with cold. I was really ill.

The next farm up the road was Sampsons Hall West and one of the Miss Partridges from there used to come in to see me and sit with me. She bought me a book and used to read to me. I used to attend their Sunday School held in a tin chapel, it was just a tin chapel on their farm. They always used to give us a little text each week, they sang gospels and Sankey hymns like 'Shall we gather at the River'. When I went to Red House it was too far to go anymore, but I loved those old hymns and I saved my Sanky hymn book and Mother would play hymns from it on Sunday nights, when we'd all sing. We would spend all evening singing, starting with hymns and then other songs. Sometimes Dad would sing some of his old Music Hall songs like 'Way went Polly with her steps so jolly that I knew she'd win'. He'd seen

The old man with his father in a rally cart

Gus Elen sing it and he'd seen Florrie Ford when he'd been round the Hall in London and he'd tell us about them.

The blacksmiths at Kersey's name was Mr Watson - there was old Mr Watson and young Mr Watson and their forge was near to Sampsons Hall. Whenever I went past to go to school I used to go in there to have a warm. He'd blow his bellows up and give me a bit of iron to tinker about with. When I grew up, I used to have my horses shod there. He used to pull my leg.

At Sampsons Hall there is a big meadow at the back of the house and orchids used to grow in there. They had spread out from the garden. They cut it for hay and of course it had these orchids in. When they fed the hay to the horses it killed two of them. They did not know that the orchids were poisonous to horses. One of the horses killed was the old man's beautiful thoroughbred hunter called Aminious. Then another horse, a grey, that had never been named and was about three years old ran into a spike. There was a piece of iron jutting out from somewhere as it ran past and that died as well. Dad never left any farm implements about in fields after that. He always had them taken out the way. It was nothing but bad luck for us at Sampsons Hall. At the back of the Hall in that orchard, there was a lot of cherry trees up one end and a beautiful mulberry tree, also some graves in there, I reckon that had been a burial ground years before. The orchids, I remember, looked something like hyacinths.

Aminious, Dad's hunter, who was poisoned by orchids that grew out of the garden at Sampsons Hall

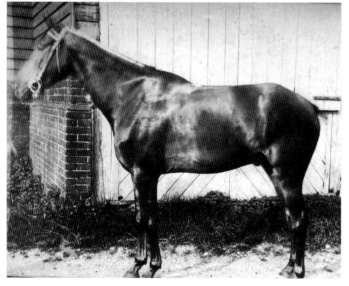

Tev Partridge's brother was killed in World War 1. Dan was the youngest member of the family. Tev Partridge had a bit shot off his chin in the war and they took a patch off his backside somewhere to put over it.

Tev and Dan used to go to a private school in Taunton, they were boarders of course. The other boy was Ginger. They were both older than me. Tev was too old to talk to me, I was only a little kid. Then there were two girls, Violet and Bessie, then younger than them was Dan and Bob. Someone used to drive a wagonette from their home in Sampsons Hall West to Kersey to take the children to school and I used to go and sit in the front with them to go to Miss Partridge's school. Dan Partridge used to keep nipping me and made me uncomfortable, he was horrible. Coming home one day, when I was old enough to ride a bicycle, he got hold of the handle bar so I couldn't move and he pushed me down into the pond.

The first year at Sampsons Hall, the old man put all the land down to peas and it was a dry summer. The peas hardly got out the ground because of the drought and we lost a lot of money. We used to collect the people from the village to come up pea picking. One day the old man said to Darkie Spooner, the foreman: "Those old gals have got big backsides Darkie, I reckon you'd better see what they've got in there". Darkie discovered that their bloomers were full up with the old man's peas so he made 'em all empty their bloomers each night before they went home. They had been putting more peas in their bloomers than they had in their sacks. Artful as a wagonload of monkeys they were.

We ploughed the land up again and put it in with potatoes the next year. The gypsies all came from miles around and camped round the corner of the fields to pick up the potatoes but that was a wet season, and the potatoes in the clamps went rotten. They used to store potatoes in clamps, that time of day. They'd put straw round them and earth on top of that to keep the frost out and they usually lasted through the winter, but this year, that was so wet, that the potatoes rotted in the clamps and the clamps kept falling in, so we lost a whole lot more money that year. Dad wasn't very pleased with that farm I can tell you.

Then there was man named Jackson, a big man, he wanted to buy a farm to give his daughter for a wedding present. She was marrying a man called Cooper, Percy Cooper, so Dad sold him

Sampsons Hall with its two hundred and something acres, I don't know how much for. Father was glad to sell it, he had two bad seasons and had lost a lot of money. He sold it for a profit to this man Cooper and we then went back to Red House Farm.

When we had moved down to Sampsons Hall, Kersey, Granddad had moved out of 'The Oblong' cottages into the Red House. Now we wanted to move back to Red House Farm Granddad then said that he would retire. He didn't want to go back to The Oblong and he was going to buy himself a house in Sudbury. He bought himself a house called Hill Crest, Clarence Road and that was right up the top of York Road. It was a very nice house, but York Road was all up hill to get up to it. He found that was too much for him to walk, to go to town and then climb this steep hill to get home, so he sold that after a while and rented another one, this time in Queens Road and that's where he lived and we moved back, of course into the Red House.

In 1914 the war broke out and in 1916, the Hollies Farm, opposite the Red House Farm was put up for sale. Mr Bridgeman was the name of the man who used to live there and when Mr Bridgeman died he had a farm manager named Harry Warboys. Corra Hills's father had had it before that. I can remember old Mr Hills, he was a real old character, he rode about with a high hat in a brougham. Harry Warboys was manager over the Hollies and he married Charlie Rainham's wife's sister. Charlie Rainham and Harry Warboys married two sisters. The girls'

Dad running a hackney stallion

name was Gardener and their father kept the paper shop in Boxford. Kathy Gardener, she was the youngest one, and Hilda Gardener was the one that Charlie Rainham married. Anyway the Hollies Farm came up for auction and the Old Man bought it and he paid £18.00 an acre for it, so we had just the Red House Farm and the Hollies Farm, farm buildings and land opposite and that's how it remained.

I was about five when we moved back to Red House Farm and I remember the day well. They drove the pigs, the cattle, the horses and all the livestock along the road and we followed on walking behind. It was a terribly hot day. Dad's foreman at Red House Farm was now Harry Tricker and he used to come up every day from Boxford. I used to walk round the farmyard with Harry Tricker, holding his hand. I used to have my breakfast sitting on the shafts of the wagon in the cart lodge with him. Mother used to give me my breakfast and I'd have it outside with Harry. He'd have a bottle of cold tea in a screw top beer bottle, a half a loaf of bread - sometimes with a pork chop or something like that on top and cut a corner off the bread for a thumb piece to go on top of the chop. Then he'd cut the bread and the chop together with his sharp knife, and eat it off the blade of the knife. Sometimes he'd just have the top of the bread scooped out and a piece of butter in.

I had to go to the barn one day to tell Dad to come in for dinner. So I went in the barn where he was and said: "Dad, dinner's all ready, come in for dinner" but he was talking to Lazzie Pattle and he didn't take any notice. "Dad will you come into dinner now? Mum says come into dinner" but he still kept on talking to Lazzie. So I got fiddling with this winnowing machine while I was waiting for him. It was a threshing machine that produces a wind across some falling seeds to blow all the light weed seed out. You turned the handle and a big cog went round a smaller cog at the bottom, and cogs ran off that to make it work. I turned the handle round, and I thought I'll stop it with the handle, then I thought I wonder if I can stop it with my fingers in the cogs, so I put my finger in the cogs and as the cogs come round so my finger went through. It split me finger down the side and flattened it out. Then in a trembling voice I said: "Dad will you come in for dinner, will you come into dinner now". He knew my voice was funny, and he looked round and saw what I had done. He picked me up and carried me out the barn. He said: "Why didn't you cry?" I said: "I couldn't because Lazzie was there."

The armband awarded to me by the Womens Land Army. I was aged 12

During the 1914-1918 War The Woman's Land Army was started. Women joined the Land Army and wore uniforms. I helped on the farm all holidays. Anyway the Chairman of the Women's Land Army saw me on top of the loads, loading and that sort of thing. She said to mother that I should join the Land Army, I was eleven years old. I couldn't have a uniform, just an armband. Some people said why give to that young but she did I was so pleased and I asked dad if he would buy me a trench coat like theirs. Dad took me to Colchester and he bought me a trench coat. It had lapels and leather buttons so I could look like a Land Army girl with my armband on.

Lazzie Pattle was having his breakfast one day. When he had finished he said to me: "You know Ruby, I've got a cork tooth".

Claude, Edna and I in muffs

I said: "You've got what? He said: "A cork tooth" - he kept on about this cork tooth. He said: "You give me your finger and I'll show you where it is in my mouth". He got hold of my hand, picked my finger up and bit it. They used to do tricks on you and things like that, but I was so furious at getting caught that he never caught me again with his 'pint of pigeon's milk' and those things.

After Miss Partridge's school I then went to Miss Byer's in Hadleigh. I was four-and-a-half years older than my sister Edna so when she was old enough to go to school at five, I had to take her down by bike as I couldn't take her if I went on my pony. Five miles there and five miles back every day on the back of my bike, I was only nine-and-a-half. She was Dad's favourite. She would not get off the bike to walk up the hill. Other children used to say: "Put her off, put her off". Well I couldn't , I used to try and push her, she'd say: "I'm not getting off." She'd say: "I shall tell Dad, I shall tell Dad." so I had to push her up every hill on my bike.

From there I went later on to Sudbury High School. They didn't have room for anymore boarders, they were full up with boarders. So I went to live with Grandma in Queens Road and Edna and Claude came too. I had to take Claude to school. He used to go to this private school - they were in the lower part of the school, so I had to look after him.

Me about the time I left school

The postman who used to bring the letters up to the farm, his name was Fred Elmer. He used to sing at all the concert parties. There were lots then and he would sing on his rounds too. I learned several of his songs because I had to go to a lot of these concert parties. Everyone used to sing them all day while they were working. Or they would whistle. The old horsemen reckoned that the horses always used to know where you were and that you were happy with them while you were singing or whistling, so they would all sing and if they went into a field together the head horseman would sing first.

> *Three men went a hunting to see what they could find*
> *First they came to a hay stack and that they left behind*
> *Said the Englishman to the Scotsman and the Scotsman he said*
> *"Nay" Befold, be fess me old grandfathers beer had blown away.*
>
> *What do you think of that now? What do you think of that now?*
> *What do you think of that now?*
> *With a whack tol-de-rol-diddle-I-day*
>
> *Three men went a hunting to see what they could find*
> *Next they came to a cow pat and that they left behind*
> *Said the Englishman to the Scotsman and the Scotsman he said 'Nay'*
> *Behold, be fess a current bun and the currents blown away*

Three men went a hunting to see what they could find
Next they came to a mile stone and that they left behind
Said the Englishman to the Scotsman and the Scotsman he said 'Nay'
Behold, be fess an old grey hare and his legs have run away

Three men went a hunting to see what they could find
Next they came to a hedgehog and that they left behind
Said the Englishman to the Scotsman and the Scotsman he said 'Nay'
Behold, be fess a pin cushion and the pins stuck in the wrong way

Then there was a song which he made up especially about the Celebrations that happened at the end of the War. They held some Celebrations down at the Rectory in Boxford and I was asked to dance and Mother came and played the piano.

Old Elmer sung "Oh what a night of jubilation" in the marquee down there. When the boys came back, they gave them a dinner. They gave him a meal afterwards - we all had one in a big marquee.

The chorus of Fred Elmer's song went:

Oh what a night of jubilation, when we hear the church bells ring
Father he was sitting in the old arm chair
Tommy and Jack will soon be back, so I don't care
Oh what an alteration, in England now by gum
All the lasses will get the sack, soon the boys will all be back
Now we know that peace days come

I was learning to dance then at Madam Bear's School of Dancing. I was learning the Highland Fling and all that sort of thing. Madam Bear came from Kensington, London and she used to come down to Hadleigh and give dancing lessons. I went to school in Hadleigh, so I used to have dancing lessons down there. Why she used to come to Hadleigh was because there was this firm as you go into Hadleigh, on the right hand side. It had a nice building, and Mr Gayford was the man that owned that building and traded there. His daughter, Eileen Gayford, went to school where I went to school and then she went onto London and she became a dancing instructor.

So they were going to give the boys a dinner and they asked me to dance at the concert. They'd got a stage rigged up and that sort of thing, Mother played the piano and I did the dancing and that is where I met George Smith. Tynott, I called him then but later when he was on the Wall of Death, he was known as Tonardo Smith. I must have been about 12. Tynott was a scout. They were doing their stuff, keeping guard. I was waiting to go in, I had my dance dress on, he had a green scout's uniform. His people then lived up at White Street Green, and George Smith, his father got his living by thatching. Then I never saw him any more for years. I was then at private school at Hadleigh and he was at the school in Boxford. The next time I met him was when we were confirmed and on Confirmation day we had to go to Edwardstone Parish Church. We went in Teddy Bowers open horse drawn carriage. There was Polly Wright and George. I was fifteen but he was younger than me. George, when he first left school, went as a mechanic for somebody, but he had a motor bike, a cracking motorbike, an AJS.

In my dancing dress when I used to dance at the old Rose and Crown in Sudbury

Charlie Rainham farmed in Ellis Street, Boxford. The Farmhouse was right on the road, a great big timbered house, a lovely old house and Charlie and his wife Hilda had two children. One was Barbara, the next one was Richard. After a dance one night down in Boxford while their mother and father were away, Richard invited us all round there to have a bacon and egg supper. I remember Richard climbing up and getting a side of bacon down off the beam and cutting it up into rashers, that was beautiful - I can taste it now.

Charlie Rainham contracted with the Council to work on the night cart and empty all the privies in the Boxford area. He didn't do it himself, he got two others to do it. One was Blinky

Claxton who came from Stone Street Road right down the far end near The Compasses. The other man was Weasel Humphrey. There's a story that they were going along and they used to have a drink at the back door of any pub on the road when they were travelling along at night to empty the privies. They just had a horse pulling an open cart with a seat across the front. One of the old boys' coats got knocked in. While he was fishing about to get it out the other one said: "You don't want to worry about that old coat. It ain't worth nothing. You'll never do anything with it if you get it out of there". "No it ain't that bor" he said "It's the might of bread and cheese I want out the pocket."

Another night Frank Waley was going home in his open sports car. They had been out again with the night cart and had a few drinks and they had hung the lamp on the wrong side of the cart. Instead of putting it on the outside, they hung the lamp on the inside. Of course Frank Waley was coming home and he saw this light and he went to overtake it, but he went straight into the back of the night cart and the stuff shot up the front, then shot back and overflowed into Frank's car. He got covered in it.

Harvesting at Charlie Raynham's Brickhouse Farm Boxford about 1943.
Photo courtesy of Adrian Tricker

When I was sixteen-and-a-half I left school. There were four of us children. We all went to private school except Tickles who

went to the village school in Boxford. He was a lot younger than us, he had his own way and regretted it later, but I don't know how we'd have found the money to send him anywhere else at that time.

When Tickles was born, we had a trained nurse in the house. Nurse Peak -Amy we all called her. On 27th March he was born and that was such a rough night. I remember Mother being upstairs and the nurse came down and said somebody's got to down for the doctor. Father said: "Ruby will have to go". It was five miles to go on a bicycle, I was only fourteen. I waited to be told that I would have to go, then the nurse came downstairs and said she could manage and the doctor could come in the morning. I had a little brother. You wouldn't think that a grown man like my Father would want to send a child of fourteen to ride 5 miles with a little oil lamp for the doctor. The doctor was always so kind to me, Dr Everett. I often had to call for him because Dad would not go. He would say: "Ru I'll put your bike in the back of my car" and I would ride back with him to the farm.

Tickles

After mother had Tickles, I don't know what was wrong with her, but not long after that she had a miscarriage. We hadn't got a maid then, so they kept me at home for one whole term from school to look after the baby. I had to look after Tickles the whole summer and I was fourteen. I used to feed him and wash him and dress him. Corra Hills used to come across and look after mother who was in bed, and the nurse used to call, but they never told me she'd had a miscarriage. I thought my mother was on the way out, that she was dying. So I carted Tickles around, and I used to sit him on my hip. I used to take him everywhere, down to the wood, it was a good long way down to the wood if you hadn't got a push cart. The men on the farm used to say: "You'll be sorry for carting him about like that, you'll have a deformed hip". Anyway I carted him about the whole summer, then I went back to school again.

Chapter 5

I started up and down from the City to the Crown
I gave me horses' water and their feed
I gave me whip a crack or two
I gave me rein a snap or two
So gip gee Darby wardee short
If you can't pull a couple a ton
I'm sure you ought
Its time we started to be home by three
Gip gee Darby gip gee gee

Sung in Boxford White Hart

Stanley Gifford gave me the first greyhound I ever had, Rear Admiral, I was about eight or nine then. He was a puppy, and had come from a man named Hales and was the cad of the litter and Stanley had it given him so he gave it to me. He always called me 'my little Ru' so he said: "My little Ru, you must keep it and train it." I called him Rear Admiral 'cause that's my initials. I kept the old dog and I trained him by walking him a lot on the road and one day they said now there's a coursing meet going to be held at Boxford. Stanley Gifford said: "You must bring your dog Ru." also Charlie Bullock was going to be there. Charlie Bullock was a great friend and a great old sportsman. He lived at Groton and used to come over and see us quite often. When I was very young and had got Royal we used to walk round on a Sunday morning, him and me with our greyhounds, to put a hare up. He showed me how to use the end of a lead and hold two dogs by putting the first finger of your right hand in the leather loop and then put it round the first greyhound's head, then back over your middle finger and round the greyhound's head again so you could hold two greyhounds with finger tip control on three fingers, and then walk out in the field with the rest of the leash in your left hand. If a hare got up you'd shout 'Lu, lu, lu' so your dog got used to that sound and knew straight away to look for a hare. You would always give the hare 'good law'. Law they called it. It was the start you let it have to

Me Edna and Admiral about the time I won my first coursing stake with him

give it a chance to run. It was usually 80 yards and called the four score law. The more the dogs were coursed, the more they would be alert. Aunt Sally, the hare, would sit right tight in her form, her little seat, and sometimes you'd walk almost on top of them before they got up. Anyhow, when you were ready you could just let your three fingers go and the dogs would be away, slipped on the hare. I have been out with them at night and put long nets in the gateways where hares run, but I stopped that because I was afraid of getting my dogs caught in the nets. Of course an old hare when its was caught would make a terrible sound, I used to hate to hear it. 'Aunt, aunt' they'd go. A mother hare, has several leverets and she'd leave them all, a long way apart, one in this field and one in another then you would see her go around from field to field and feed them - just once a day. It's wonderful how they seemed to spread their chances of survival. When you are out with the slipper at a coursing meeting, sometimes if you had a dog that did not like walking next to another one, it would get the wrong side of it and backwards, so they had to lift the dog right over. Then they got some better slips somehow, with bigger collars and that had one central lead with a rope coming up the middle. You would pull a thing on the end and that had a mechanical device there so that unlocked both the collars together and away the dogs would go. One would have a red collar on and one a white collar on, the red collar was always the top dog, it was so you could tell the dogs apart.

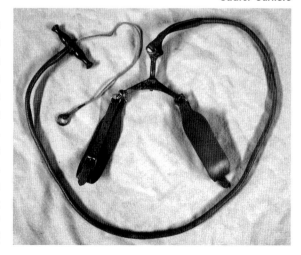

a pair of coursing slips stamped Sewell Sadler Carlisle

It didn't matter if a greyhound was first up to the hare. That one wasn't always the winner. It was the one that turned the hare the most times. Turning the hare means getting close enough to make it break away at an angle. There were more points for the first dog to get up to the hare. They did not always catch the Hare and if they did catch one it was taken away and humanely killed quickly and given to one of the followers for a dinner. Old Lazzie Pattle always seemed to be one of the first there. People took from nature then but only what they needed and nothing was wasted. They had more respect for nature in those days. If you saw a big covey of English Grey Partridges you'd always count them, sometimes there'd be as many as 18. I've seen the old man stop his car to count a covey of partridges and that would be a topic of discussion at dinner.

The judge at coursing meets would be on horseback along with one or two others and they would help put the hare up. The judge in the Sudbury and District was always Mr Charlie 'Bumper' Kemble. There were three Kemble brothers, Fred, William and Charlie. Charlie was our neighbour. He married Betty Kemble and he lived at Cox Farm. She had two single sisters and they were single when they died. The sisters lived in Boxford with their father and mother in Butchers Lane. Fred Kemble lived at Groton Hall: his housekeeper's name was Miss Govett, a very prim and proper little person. Everyone said that he slept with his housekeeper so one night when the boys left The Fox at Gorton, some of them went round to Fred Kembles house and shouted out 'Fire....... Fire.' Up went the window in a hurry and they all saw two heads came out of the same window.

I am standing second from the right in the coat that I unpicked every seam of and turned inside out

COURSING AT BILDESTON 1923

Charlie Bullock had an unusual thing. Both of his two middle fingers of his hands were joined together. At Poplar Farm where Charlie Bullock lived, just down the Hollies Lane at the end, we would go there in the Winter time with a lantern because he loved to play cards. When we went there, the card game we nearly always played was 'three halfpenny loo' and I've never heard it played anywhere else, but that must have been very popular in its day because there are all these antique Victorian loo tables that were made it seems to play it on.

I belonged to the Sudbury and District Coursing Club. I joined it when I had my first dog. They'd meet at Boxford and all the other local places. You had to join if you wanted to course. I was also a member of the Colchester and District Coursing Club. I'm on that photo of the Sudbury & District meet in Bildeston in 1923 in the coat that Mother had made for me in Harris Tweed. I wore and wore it till it was worn to a frazzle and I couldn't wear it any more 'cause it was dirty looking so I took it all to pieces and turned it and restitched it. I was only a kid of 18.

Greyhound Stud 1918

Sudbury & District Coursing Club 28 January 1913

HOLD ON III. (33), bk, '10 (Makin), by Free Ferry—Peninsula.
Happy Midget (30), w bd. '10 (Hale), by Lord Drake—Such a Mite.
Rear Admiral II., bd w d, April, '16; Miss R. Alleston.

HOME RULE IV. (31), r f, '11 (Hayes), by Fight for Freedom—Revolving Light.

CLUB CUP STAKES (Club), for all ages, that have run in a stake at any previous meeting of the present season, at 10s. each ; winner, cup value £4. 4s and £1; second £2; 16 subs.

Mr H. E. Bacon's bd d *Glenfire*, by Glenfield—Maid o' the Mist (1)	beat	Mr P. H. Oliver's w bk d *Hop On IV.*, by Mandini—Stanhope
Mr H. E. Scarff's bk d *Butley Bridge*, by Butley Nigger—Butley Maggie	„	Mr B. R. Mayor's bd b *Matchmaker*, by Glacier — Grateful Jean
Mr J. W. Baker's f d *Kennett Jim*, by Glenfield — Lovely Morn	„	Mr B. Steed's bd d *White Hasssock*, by White Rubicon—Hazy Morn
Mr R. B. Smith's bd b *Sins of Society*, by Waldegrave—Wicken Lass	„	Mr F. C. Steed's bd b *Flo Dove*, by Cobduck—Dancing Dia
Mr G. Springett's bd b *Gay Sally* (1. Boyton Belle), by Bewcastle—Wallflower	„	Mr V. Hill's r w b *Very Hopeful*, by Such a Sell—Wicken Lass (1)
Mr H. A. Frith's bd d *Bachelor*, by Briers Hey—Bibelot	„	Mr H. E. Scarff's bk d *Hadleigh Darkie* (1. Nightmare), by Royal Foe—Wonder's Substitute

I used to buy Lavenham Tweed from a man named Bill Jarvis. He lived in Water Street, Lavenham. You'd go into his room and he'd say: "What colour would you like?" If you said: "Red, white and blue". He'd do you a bit of cloth in all those colours. He could make anything up you wanted. It was a bit like a Harris Tweed, but better than that. The whole of the room was all different coloured wool. I used to call there and take him a little bit of Mother's home-made butter. It didn't make any difference to what he charged me, he only charged 5/- a yard and a yard was 27 inches wide. He had a loom in there and used to weave it all himself. He was the last of those old weavers and had worked in Ropers who had the last big mill in Lavenham. So he really was the last of the Suffolk Weavers who brought the prosperity to Lavenham. I still have some of his tweed now - you couldn't wear it out. Then his son took over and that all finished when he got fined for passing some Harris Tweed off as Lavenham.

Anyway Charlie Bullock was gonna be at this coursing meet at Boxford, I knew he'd tell me what to do, so I went down there with Dad. There was a man named Squirrel, he was a builder, and had got a very good greyhound whose name was Music, and I heard Music was gonna be there. I hadn't got the proper stuff for my dog, I hadn't got the gear, I hadn't got a rug or a leather lead so I took him on the chain that he used to be chained up with. So I arrived down at the coursing meeting and I'd got this little chain you see. They all told me was I must make some collars. You had to have a red collar or a white collar, top dog and bottom dog and I didn't have a collar at all, I just took him on his chain. They looked at my old dog, theirs all had rugs on and he didn't have a rug and Oh they did laugh. I couldn't keep up with them walking either, because they'd walk

across field after field before they'd kick up a hare. I wasn't big enough to walk all these miles for hares. As we were walking along to put a hare up, Charlie Bullock said: "I'll look after your dog for you Ruby."

I forget who Admiral was drawn against the first time, but he won his first course, then it came to the second round, and be blowed, if he didn't win his course again the second round. Then he was in the final and I was drawn against Music, belonging to Charlie Squirrel, so he had this third course and damn it if Admiral didn't run away with it and he won. So I won the course, I'd won the stake. The stake in those days was only 25 shillings, we'd all put five bob in the hat. I was not old enough to go in the pub when we'd finished and they all congregated. It was down at The Swan so I waited outside, then they called me in to collect my money and they gave me my 25 bob and my father said to me "Well you'd better walk home to Red House Farm 'cause I'm not coming home yet." I'd been walking all day, walked as far as the dog. Anyway, the old man stayed down there with the rest of the coursing folk and I couldn't go in the pub so I'd got old Admiral on his chain and set out to walk home on my own. Mr Bullock was nice to me and said: "I'll see you have a rug for him next time you bring him out". I then walked across the road into Mrs Munsan's sweet shop and I bought Old Admiral two penny worth of jube jubes, he loved jube jubes that old dog did, then I walked back up Cox Hill to Red House Farm, about two miles.

Tickles and Edna

Next week I went up to Ipswich on the bus, and I went into Alfred Clarke's, the saddlers. I went in there and I said I wanted a greyhound rug. They brought some out to show me and they were a lot of money. They were more money than I had got. I'd only won 25 bob, but I did manage to buy him a navy blue one with yellow binding round in the end. Then I saved up my money to buy him a leather lead, so next time I took him coursing he'd look the part. Unfortunately something happened at home, I don't know what happened, but we heard a terrible yelp one night in the yard, 'cause he was let loose at night time to be on guard. When I got up next morning, I went to look for my dog, and he was dead lame, something had struck him across the shoulder and his shoulder was out and he was never any more good, poor old boy. I reckon someone was prowling about the yard and saw him, but he'd still catch a rabbit on his three legs. If I'd had known what I know now, I'd have taken him straight to a vet and said can you put his shoulder back, but times were hard then and there was no money about and Dad wouldn't take him to a vet or anything like that.

Charlie Bullock had got a little bitch called Baseball and she was a very good little bitch. He wanted to breed from her, so he took old Admiral over there. Instead of money passing between you, it was usual for the owner of the dog to have the pick of the litter. Eventually Baseball had some puppies by old Admiral, Admiral was a brindle and white and she was a bluey colour. Charlie Bullock kept a little blue puppy and he called it Blueball and he gave me one, I was supposed to have

the pick of the litter as Admiral was the sire, so I picked the one that had got the biggest white leg at the front the first time I saw the puppies. I thought I'll have that one, that was brindle and had a nice white leg. Now one was sold to Stanley Gifford and when they were old enough and he went to collect his he said he'd bring mine back for me. When my little dog came, I didn't realise it was the wrong one when he bought her over, and when I saw Stanley Gifford's, I thought blast, that's the one I picked out, it had got a white leg and he named it Solid Gold and that was the best of the lot. My little bitch was a good little bitch though. Charlie Bullock taught me a lot about greyhounds. He used to tell me tales about before the 1914-18 war going to buy greyhounds at Adridges Auction in the Barbican in London.

When she was old enough I had my little bitch out to a coursing meeting held at Boxford and they went down to Peyton Hall and there was a hundred-acre field at Peyton Hall. A hundred-acre field is a bad thing to run a dog on because you can very likely slip a dog onto a hare and by the time that's coursed the hare and finished, another hare would jump up somewhere and the dogs would go after that. A dog will run and finish itself and lay down and die sometimes, run itself right out. So you want to be there to get hold of your dog as soon as its finished coursing. This was a puppy stakes and mine was called Royal Act, my initials again. It won its first course and it won its second course in the puppy stakes and I was well pleased. There was a man named Braybrook from Sudbury who'd got a dog who'd also done the same thing, he'd won two courses, same as mine. In the second course my little dog ran in, it got cut and it was terribly lame. I wouldn't have run her but you don't want to have your dog beaten. Run and beaten. So I went up to Mr Braybrook to ask him to divide the stake, which you do if you have bad luck and you can't compete. So I went to Mr Braybrook, who had a milkround in Sudbury and I said: "Mr Baybrook, I can't run my little dog". It was a puppy, not an old dog, even more you want to take care of a puppy. So I said to him "I can't run my little dog because she's cut herself badly." I said "Will you divide with me, divide the stake. So he said: "No. If your bloody dog can't run, withdraw it." That was the only thing I could do, but I didn't want my dog's record tarnished. So he said, "No. If you can't run your dog," he said, "withdraw it".

So I said: "I shan't withdraw it" I says "I'll see yer, I'll run her." So I went back to old Charlie Bullock and told him. He said: "I'll tell you what I'll do," and he said "Hold that foot up" and he had some stuff on that deadens the pain and to stop her bleeding and he put that on it. The little bitch was still a bit lame. You could get 10 to 1 against my dog, 10 to 1 that it would be beaten, and I walked up as close as I could walk to that side to pick it up when the course was over, you see I didn't want it to walk with a gammey leg and this all happened on this hundred-acre field. We walked up, and the slipper was Squirrel from Bildeston. I went up to him and I said: "Don't give her too much law." If you don't know what 'too much law' is, it means don't let the hare get too far away before you slip 'em. I wanted a short course for my little dog you see, I wanted her to go out and kill it and that's that. He said: "I won't give it too much law, I'll look after it". Everybody thought it was very sporty to run the dog. Anyway he slipped the dog onto the hare and I'm damned if she didn't lead the other dog up to the hare. She led the other dog and won the course, she led that other dog about 2 lengths. I went to pick up my dog and Braybrook was there to pick up his dog. I picked my dog up and I looked at him and I said: "How do you like your new master?" I never did get on with old Braybrook after that.

Eventually I wanted to breed from my dog, Royal, so I sent her down to the Black Bull at Sudbury, where Harry Harper had got a good stud greyhound. They took her in and put her in a stable but she escaped. They rang up and said that my dog was out and they didn't know where she was. I went nearly mad. Anyway I couldn't find her so I put an advertisement in the paper, in the East Anglian Daily Times, to say she was lost. After about two weeks I heard from the Allestons (the same name as ours, but only distant relatives and who farmed at Little Waldingfield) that there had been a greyhound seen in that area. I got on my little two-stroke motor bike. Hec Tricker - who looked after the cows came with me on his bike and we went over to Waldingfield; we looked around and damned if we didn't see her. We called to her and she ran right past us into the road and I saw her jump a five-bar gate and go into a field. Her coat stared and was caked with mud, she looked real poor - well she had been away a fortnight. I watched her go right across the field away from us. I said to Hec: "I don't know what we can do." We went back so we got round behind this field. We were thinking about going home because we couldn't see her anymore and couldn't do anything because she wouldn't come when we called her. She didn't recognise us any more, so I started my motor bike up to go home and that made a putt, putt, putt sound. I was towing Hec along 'cause he was on his pedal bike, when all of sudden something came over this big high fence into the road. It was her, she had recognised the putt-putt of my motorbike. I caught her and made a fuss of her, of course she then knew who I was and I took her home on a lead beside Hec's bike. I went ever so steady and that took a long time, because we were seven or eight miles from home. I said: "She'll never go off the farm any more" and neither she did. She used to run loose around the farm though and she'd try and get in my bedroom. She did breed another a brindle bitch and I called her Royal the Second and when this one was quite old Tickles had her covered and she gave birth to Prem and Light, his two dogs.

Royal Act and I

Hec Tricker was Harry Tricker's nephew. He was a very willing boy. My greyhounds ate his dinner once. He used to bring his dinner up in a white linen bag. I think it was Admiral that ate it. He came up to the door and he said to Mother: "The greyhound's eaten all my grub for the day." She said: "Oh dear Hec. How much did you have? I'll get you something for your dinner".
He said "Bread and cheese, bread and butter, half a herring and a slice of cake". That same boy, when the cows were chained up to the manger, rode the bull. There were about two dozen cows and when you let them out to the meadow you had to undo the chain. When it came to the last one it was a bull and one day Hec jumped on the bull's back, undone the chain and the bull went off at full gallop,

galloped round the yard they were in then down through the mud towards the pond. When he came to the pond he stopped dead and chucked Hec off right over his head into the pond. I wonder it didn't gore him because he was a nasty bull. A lovely looking bull, but he was savage.

I had a big dog called Golden Twilight and I bought him off Bogie Bowtell the bookmaker from Sudbury. He originally belonged to George Thurlow, the steam engine and threshing tackle dealer from Stowmarket, and he was trained by Harry Aggis at Stowmarket. He sold him because he broke a toe and they thought he would never be able to run any more. I contacted Bogie Bowtell somehow and he sold him to me for four pounds. His toe never did affect him though. I ran him once or twice and I won one or two stakes with him. Aggis used to have a Pork Butcher's shop just over the water splash in Kersey where Frank Gage's mother lived and also had one in Hadleigh. He moved to take a pub in Stowmarket.

If we went to play cards with Chris Bullock we would always play 'three halfpenny loo'. I'll tell you how to play, first of all you deal the cards out. You have three cards each and the last card that you deal out you turn up for trumps. If your hand isn't good enough you can throw it in. The person sitting next to the dealer leads and there had to be two of you left in and if everybody else chucks in and one person is still staying in then the dealer had to play. When there's three people left in and each one wins a trick that's a 'Kromas titum', because everyone has one. Then when the dealer deals they deal a spare hand and the person next to the dealer has the option of taking it, changing his hand for the 'titum hand'. If he doesn't take it the next person has the option and so on. It must have been ever so popular in its day because of all those loo tables but it had so many peculiar rules so I suppose that's why it died out.

Chapter 6

What's the life of a man any more than a leaf

As I was a-walking one morning in spring
A viewing the fields and to hear the birds sing
A thought came in mind as I wandered along
Like the leaves we shall wither and sooner and soon shall be gone

CH
What's the life of a man any more than a leaf?
A man has his seasons, then why should he grieve?
Although in this wide world he appears fine and gay
Like the leaf he shall wither and soon fade away

You should have seen the leaves but a short time ago
They were all in full motion appearing to grow
Till the frost came and bit them, and withered them all
And the storm came upon them and down they did fall

Down in yonder churchyard many names you will see
That have fallen from this world as the leaves from the tree
Old age and affliction upon them did fall
And death and disease came and blighted them all.

Mother always had a 'mother's help' in the house and they were something busy. I used to give a hand with things here but mostly I had to be out working on the land. Almost everything in the house was home-made in those days; there was hardly anything bought at shops apart from the raw provisions. There were no sinks with drains, or anything like that. The water had to be brought in from outside.

Outside the backdoor on the right as you were coming in was a big place called the back kitchen and that had the water pump in it with a big, long, iron handle. There were two coppers in there and the floor sloped down to a gully that run right the way through. If you killed a pig you could cut it up in there as you

Felixstowe Tart

Mix 4 ozs Cornflour 4 ozs Flour,
(or all flour & &), 1 small teaspoon-
ful baking powder, 1 Tablespoonful
Castor Sugar, rub in 3 ozs butter
or lard. Beat up yolk of egg.
with sufficient milk to mix it
(about 2 tablespoonfuls) lightly roll
out this dough & cover well
greased dinner plate leave
edges thicker & crimp with thumb
Bake biscuit brown in hot
oven. Then fill with raspberry
or other preserve & pour over
white of the egg beaten to
a stiff snow with two tablespoonfuls Castor Sugar. Put
in a cool oven to set

K. W.? Receipt

could wash the whole place down. One copper was for washing and the other for brewing. Both on either side of the fire that also had a Dutch oven. Mother, Cack as we called her because she cackled so much, used to put faggots in there and bake bread and cakes in the early days.

They brewed regularly on the farm that time of day; usually Harry Tricker did it, then he would bring it in and store it in two large barrels that Dad had bought. They used to have Port Wine in them and they put them down in the little game cellar. That was a sort of half-cellar with about eight steps down. When they put these port barrels in they were so big that they had to take the windows out. When Harry left, Billy Simpson did it regularly. He brewed some lovely beer and would make some for the Italian prisoners of war. They made him a wicker work filter and I still have it. They used to distill wheat wine into a Whisky. Billy Simpson's beer was always known as Hoom Brewed and even the cousins from London when they came down would ask for Billy Simpson's Hoom Brewed. Billy said that he had always brewed the beer on the farm that he was on. It used to be the boy's job and the old men had told him not to use pump water but oily looking water out of the horse pond with weevils in it. You had to scrape them off the surface and if a horse died on the farm they might hang a leg in it for it to feed on and become stronger but we asked him not to do that to ours. He always sent a barrel up to the house at harvest and brewed another for the men.

Dad didn't drink a lot really but he still used to buy his whisky by the gallon from Olivers in Bury St. Edmunds. His favourite bottled beer was oatmeal stout, made by Wards of Foxearth, he said that was the best beer in England and he was right, too, because they won more gold medals than anyone - even Guinness. We had no mains water but Ward's beer was delivered to the door. Dad used to drink milk, there was so much of it. He said that if they served it in pubs he would only drink milk. He used to go out and get tight occasionally, particularly when he was younger. I remember once when we had to get him home from The Fleece, coming past the Police Station, he would insist on ringing the Police bell and he was lucky not to get run in.

Receipt for Pickling Hams
20 lbs & over.

1 lb Pickling Salt -
1/2 lb Bay Salt -
2 oz Salt Petre.
1 lb Pickling Ham Sugar.

Method. Powder the Bay Salt, Salt Petre, & Salt, mix together & rub well into the Ham, lay in Pickling Pan, and do ones awards alright, next day take
1 Pint Stout -
1/2 Pint Vinegar
& 1 lb Sugar - Boil these & pour over the Ham. Boiling hot & well baste until nearly cold, turn every day for one month - (Hang up to dry.)
(Fanny Warren.)

In this back kitchen they used to do all sorts of jobs. If you were going hunting you'd get the horse harness out in there the night before, ready for an early start. Take an oil lamp out and get it all ready, all your harness and everything, and treat it all with saddle soap and neatsfoot oil. At Christmas time, that was where they'd pluck the chickens and turkeys. I've seen a mass of feathers piled up to the roof, so you could hardly get in. The men would be in there a singing if they were working late. Dad would make sure that they had a pint or two of beer. The lead pump in this outside kitchen was hard work and all the water in the house had to be got in. It all had to be pumped up by hand.

The wicker work beer filter made by Billy Simpson for the Italian prisoners of war

I remember Edna squirting some water at me and I squirted some back, and she said: 'I'll tell Dad". Well, the next thing was he came in there after me and I was ready for him. I had a bucket of water and when he tried to give me a thick ear I threw that at him. Well, he chased me out and about, upstairs, but I got away from him though. I got out of my bedroom window onto a corrugated iron roof over the back door and he daren't get out on there! I'd jump off. I often had to escape from him like that.

Another time when he chased me, I got out through the window that way, then I got my bike and I went up the road and that was getting dark. When the men came up the road they said to me: "Watch out Ru, he's after you, and he's coming up the road" I got over the gate into Morleys Meadow and ran across and got back into the garden and into the house and I hid up. The fence I got through had been done up, a wattle fence. I got over it somehow. Dad saw me go across the meadow and came across the meadow after me 'cause he thought I should be hung up in that fence. He went up to the fence and gave it such a good hiding he knocked it all down.

Summer Pickle.
for Beef.

1 Gallon of Water.
1/2 lb loaf Sugar.
1/2 oz Salt Petre.
1 lb Salt.
Boil these together to
dissolve, when the Beef
Comes from Butchers, rub
well with Salt, & let it
remain 2 days, then wipe
dry, & put into the prepared
Cold pickle.
(Mrs E. Partridge)

Just inside the backdoor, on the right-hand side, was the dairy and then beyond that on the right-hand side was this little game cellar, and on the left was the big kitchen where we all used to eat. In the dairy either side there were long deal trestles where there were big skimming pans that they'd put the milk in and then they'd fleet the cream off. Mother used to keep the cream and once a week she would make butter with it in the churn. These big shallow pans were about 3ft. across. The new ones were enamel, but her mother's were the old ones that were earthenware. She would also use them all for curing hams. At the end of the room were two great big wooden safes with wire grilles on. Underneath there were always earthenware pickling troughs. In one she'd be pickling eggs to eat during the winter, when the hens weren't laying. They used to pickle them in some stuff called 'waterglass' but you couldn't use that pot any more, because that used to put fur round the inside. You could only use it for eggs again. Once she'd put these eggs in this waterglass you couldn't boil them and eat them like fresh eggs, you could only use them for cooking. Eggs were most expensive then. We used to laugh about Mrs. Beeton's Cookery Book that said take so many eggs, because you just couldn't afford them then. Eggs were really expensive, and so was a chicken. A chicken was a lot of money, that was more money then than that is now. We used to eat all of it. Mum would put the chicken legs in boiling water, scald them and skin the scales off them and use them to make gravy with the giblets.

She used to buy a brisket or flank of beef, a whole one at a time, and put it in pickling bowls. It would keep it there for a month or two, and then she'd just cut a piece off when we wanted it. It would be pickled in brine and then she just used to cook it so that we could have boiled beef and carrots. Things like refrigerators were unheard of but they had their own ways of keeping things. She also used to pickle ox-tongue and

(Very good K. Wann-Key

Christmas Cakes.

1/2 lb Butter or marg.
1/2 lb Sugar -
work there together with a wooden spoon, until sufficiently soft. then lightly beat it until it resembles whipped Cream.
Add — 5 Eggs one at a time's beating well each time's
Stir in 1 lb Sultanas
        1/2 Currants. 1/2 lb Stoned
Plums, 4 oz Candied Peel

1/4 lb Citron, Sweet Almond & 2 g of Candied Cherrys. 1 grated nutmeg, lastly add
3/4 Flour, plain, + teaspoon Baking Powder, bake well in moderate Oven, & will keep 6 months in an tight Tin.

71

we always had one ready at Christmas to eat with a cured ham that she'd boil specially.

When we killed a pig, that used to be brought into the back kitchen and laid on a pig bench. That was sliced right through in two halves and almost everything would be saved and eaten. The head and parts of the body would be cut up and made into brawn and sausages. Then there was the chitterlings. There were lovely fried. That's the pig's intestine but they had to be cleaned in salt water and turned a number of times. All the pig fat would be 'tried' down. They'd try it down into lard for cooking with, in a great big pan by heating it all up and Mother used to take the crispy bits that were left out of there and mix them with some currants in a pastry and make some nice little cakes. We called 'em rock cakes, they were very rich. Pig lard was not for dripping - it was for cooking with and pastry. Dripping generally comes from cooking a joint of beef, where you save all

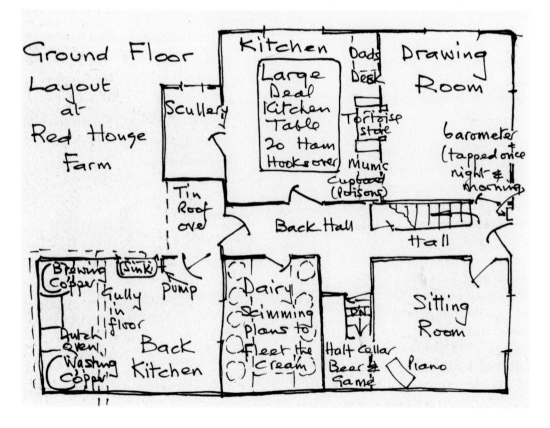

the fat and then you can have that for breakfast on toast with some pepper and salt. We also used to have what we called 'kettle broth'. This was bread with hot water on it, strained off and then mixed with a bit of butter or dripping, pepper and salt or you could have milk on it and sugar instead as a milk sop, or ferret sop as Tickles named it. You might have half a cold pig's trotter for breakfast and you'd peel the skin off and pick out the bits of meat in between. Things like cornflakes and those manufactured things we never ever had.

If milk went sour Mother would drain it in muslin and she'd put currants in it sometimes to eat as a cream cheese. I still have Mother's recipe book. She didn't put everything in it as most things were carried in her head. Absolutely nothing came out of a printed book. Everything that she wrote in her recipe book she always wrote down the name of the person she got it from, she knew the source then, and how good that was. She wouldn't ever have used a recipe like out of Mrs Beaton's book.

Boxford Street with
Ru walking horse
next to Rules bus

Broad Street, Boxford. J 5310. (Clarke's Ser

Tickles and Chas. Alleston, Winifred Dawson, Laura Riddlesdell, Frank Dawson, Helen Riddlesdell, Mark Riddlesdell, Miss Steward, Frith Dawson, Ruby, Bert Cook and Arthur Riddlesdell

Mother's home cured hams were renowned everywhere and they'd all ask for her recipe, but she wouldn't give it away. A chef we knew was doing a very special dinner in the war years in London and he kept coming up and plaguing Mother for one of her hams. Eventually she let him have one. After the dinner Lord Iveagh sought out the chef. He went round afterwards to find the chef to see if he could buy some 'cause he said that was the best he'd ever tasted. Hers was different from others. It was made with stout, again we always had Wards oatmeal stout. They used to get the pigs as big as possible, about 15 or 16 score live weight. They only have them at little more half that weight now. Years before they used to have them even bigger - sometimes 20 score hogs. Then they would cut the hams on the round across the top which made the ham bigger, not square like they do today. The first thing mother did when she got'em was rub saltpetre round the joint at the top, cos if they went bad they always went bad round that joint, so you had to rub that well in right the way round the joint. After pickling she used to hang these hams up to drip and when dry. They would be put in a pillowcase and hung over the top of the kitchen table - the big scrubbed deal table that used to be in the middle of the kitchen. There was about a dozen or more hooks specially for hams and bacon. I've seen 5 or 6 hams hang up there, also sides of bacon and cured chaps. They'd hang there for a year. If you had'em before six months they were called a green ham and they weren't really ready. They were ideally cured at Michaelmas, which is the eleventh of October in Suffolk, to be eaten after haysel or the following Lady day. She got her secrets from her mother, Fanny Warren. That was her recipe.

She used to cook everything on the old iron Tortoise stove in the kitchen and I can see that frying pan now sizzling on the iron hake that dropped down in front and the smell of her bacon and sausages - well there was nothing like it. They made lovely brawn too. I suppose we were lucky having so much milk. We used to feed the skimmed milk to the pigs, and mother's butter was sought after as well. We always had Red Poll cows and their milk was very rich. You'd have to scald the churn out thoroughly first, and then keep winding, until you felt the butter come. That was an arm aching old job. With the cream she'd make horseradish sauce by just getting horseradish out of the verges and washing then grating it up and mixing with vinegar, cream, salt and pepper and a little mustard. Salad dressing the same. She was also renowned for her Christmas puddings, they'd keep over a year as well, we've eat them two years old - they seemed to taste even better. That was her mother's recipe again. We didn't used to have 'em just at Christmas, we'd have 'em for birthdays, and they always slipped a little silver three penny piece in a piece of greaseproof paper, as that was lucky if you got it. She used to boil several at a time in the outside copper. And, oh, her mince pies, they were good! She always made them when it was getting towards Christmas in case anyone came in you could offer them a mince pie and a glass of sherry. Another thing that everyone liked was her shortbread. That recipe came from Sue Cady, she was the baker's wife down in Boxford. Mr Cady used to bake bread in the morning and in the afternoon she used to bake cakes in the oven as that was still hot. Mother gave up baking bread when she could get it from Mr Cady, who used to come round with it. Sue Cady's shortcakes were reckoned the best. They sold them for a penny halfpenny each.

Shortcakes (Sue Cady)

Sue Cady was the baker in Boxford and was renowned for her cakes and shortcake.

Into 1lb self raising flour rub
6oz lard (or lard and butter) and make into pastry with milk
Roll out pastry and work into it
¼lb of sugar
2oz currants. Rollout and cut into shapes

Easter morning when we came down to breakfast mother always had boiled eggs already for us with painted faces on.

Ellis Street Boxford. The steps in the middle were where I used to take rabbits up to Weasel Humphrey

Dad would have cold pork and cold parsnips, or greens or brussel sprouts with vinegar on for his supper, and he used to insist on eating his pudding in the old fashioned way. That was

Boxford. Ellis Street. (Clarke's Series.)

a boiled batter pudding not like the Yorkshire ones that rise up. That was boiled, steamed in the water, and then he'd have that with the gravy on first and the main meal to follow. That's the real old way.

If we had any spare rabbits to sell, we'd take them down to Charlie Humphrey in Boxford. He lived in a little cottage near Johnny Whymark's Garage in Ellis Street opposite the Greenbanks Dairy. He used to deal in them and he'd send them up to be sold in Sudbury market. You could send almost anything on the buses then, either Rule's or Corona. One day a whole lot of ferrets got out that someone had sent and all of the ladies had to jump on their seats while the conductor got em back. There was a story about Jack Stiff taking a calf to send to Ipswich market on the bus but they wouldn't take that. They would hold up the Hadleigh train for Frank Gage who used to send goats up to London for the Kosher trade. If a cat or something was pregnant the men would say 'its like the Corona bus - got passengers inside' or they'd say 'its been to the whist drive'.

Johnny Whymark outside his garage in Ellis Street, Boxford. Photo courtesy of Adrian Tricker

About an hour before dusk the Mother's help would put a big oilcloth on the table and then get all the oil lamps out and trim the wicks, then put new mantles on the Tilley and fill them up. A Tilley lantern, that had pumped up pressure, was a new thing. I bought one off old Mr Barrel, the butcher then, he was Bert Cooke's boss, and I gave him seven and sixpence for it. All we had were one or two lamps of an evening wherever we were so you could do a bit of needlework. I used to do a bit of smocking, drawn thread work and we used to make all our own dresses and petticoats.

If you went to the toilet outside at night you always took a lamp with you. A candle, or something like that when you went up to bed.

Everyone in the house had a brass bedstead. They were 4ft. standard size and you had them whether you were single or whether there were one or two in the bed. You quite often had to share a bed with someone if they came to stay. You'd have a feather mattress on top because they were so warm. They came up all around you and held the warmth in the feathers. There was a marble top washstand in every room with a jug and basin on it. Every morning you'd have to wash in that cold water, that and a bit of Palmolive soap. Sometimes there was ice on the top.

Cora Hills, who married Leonard Underwood, in her Land Army outfit

The windows were often iced up on the inside in winter. You had to take your own slop pail out in the morning. It either went down the toilet or into the back ditch.

They had some funny old cures that time of day. If you got whooping cough they used to give you fried mouse. Fried mouse they'd give you. I never had any myself I'm glad to say, I never had whooping cough, but they reckon that would cure you, I can't think how that did.

When I had an ulcer in my mouth Mother gave me Bitter Aloes. Tincture of Arnica was what they'd put on if you had to bring a bruise out. And if you hit your foot with a bit of metal or ran a fork into it, we would always grease the piece of metal afterwards. They reckoned that stopped you getting lockjaw. If you had a boil they used to put a poultice on it and how they made that poultice was to get a piece of sheet and put some bread in it, then pour boiling water on it and squeeze it out. Then put a spoonful of sugar inside it and fold it up and put that on the boil, because that would draw it. If you had a boil on the back of your neck they'd get a strong little bottle, put boiling water in it, tip it out and put the neck of the bottle over the boil straight-away and that would draw it as well. I have heard of people making them go away by squeezing huslick on them. When you had a bad cold on your chest, Mother always rubbed camphorated oil on it till you could taste it and they'd make you some linseed tea. They'd get a pound of linseed, wash it, put it in a pot and boil it. After it has been strained through muslin it goes like jelly and they used to dissolve some Spanish liquorice in it and you would take a wine glass full. I still buy Spanish liquorice in a stick and cut it up and have lumps of that for my throat. If you have a cold on the chest there's nothing like it for moving the phlegm, nothing like it. Another good cough mixture we had mixed up was 6 drams of chlordine, 1 ounce of glycerine, 4 pennyworth of ipecacuana wine and 4 ounces of liquorice, diluted in equal parts of water.

If you had a wart, Cora Underwood was the one for getting rid of them. She'd say "Let me look at your wart" and you'd show it to her, and she'd say "How many have you got?" That was all she'd ask, then in a week or so that wart would disappear. Cora was married to Leonard Underwood and they had a small farm at Castlings Heath. They would come over regularly to play cards of an evening.

Mother used to rub our chests with camphorated oil but that was poison, so you had to be careful not to drink it or let an animal drink it, and you had to be careful putting it somewhere that was a bit tender. Mother's recipe for Hoss Oils was good and we used that if we had a sprain or pain in the back or such like. Tickles put some on in the bath and that ran down the small of his back until that reached his tender most where he gave out a mighty yell. We heard his call in the sitting room when he was having his bath in front of the Tortoise Stove in the Kitchen. If anyone had a bath that was a rare job as you had to heat all the water in all the pots, kettles and saucepans that you could find on the old Tortoise Range. That all came out the water butt cause that was soft water and you often had a few floating weevils in it. Mum's embrocation would draw a bruise or anything like that out. You couldn't beat it.

They did have some funny old cures that time of day. I remember an old horseman telling me how they used to charm a horse with the frog's bone and another said he had his own special mixture that was guaranteed to charm a horse. That was 'oil of cumin, oil of man, black drops three drops.' I never knew anything about those things, most of the horses I had responded to kindness, I always talked to my dogs and horses. I remember when we had a dog with distemper, we put a rope round it with Stockholm tar on it and that got over it. They used to say that if a horse had navicular, which you couldn't cure, (it's where a bone grows in the foot), the travellers and others used to tether them to a stream of running water overnight so they were numb before they sold them or if they had a big place on the foot they would walk them through mud so they had caked mud all over their hooves and you couldn't see it when they went in the sales.

Dad hated mice, he couldn't bear them. Once when he was down where they were threshing, of course there were no end of rats and mice, and a mouse ran up his trouser leg and he went frantic. He was throwing off his overcoat and jacket and waistcoat. The men came running and Billy Simpson saw that move underneath his shirt and he put his hand down there, bang and killed it, squashed it underneath his shirt where that was. Then he had to get it out.

People didn't move far that time of day, because there wasn't the transport to get about. There was a Mr N S Rule of Broad Street, Boxford; he had been an insurance agent. He bought a bus. I can't remember what sort that was. He had a coal round as well. The top of the bus used to come off. They'd raise that off on pulleys and then he'd use the buck for delivering coal in the daytime. On a Thursday, he'd put the top back on again and people would get in to go to Sudbury for market day. Eventually they got several buses and became a big company. They moved to Riverside House in Broad Street. That's the other side of the river that runs next to the street and there's a bridge over it. The river goes shallow there. I've seen Mr Rule snare a pike or two out of the river from the bridge.

I had some rabbits when I was a young girl at Red House Farm. I had two Dutch rabbits and a Belgium hare. One night two of them went missing, that only left me with the Belgium hare and they couldn't think where they'd gone. Someone had taken them and they discovered it was an old man that worked on the farm had come back at night and got them. I suppose he had eaten them. Dad wasn't very pleased about that at all and I was upset. I then bought another rabbit off Jim Hood. His father was the manager of the mat factory in Sudbury and that cost me shillings. He said it was a doe so when it was ready I took it to the buck. Does don't bang on the bottom of the cage like the bucks do, but they will bang on the bottom of the cage when they are ready for the buck. There was banging on the bottom of the cage, so I thought that must be ready. Someone said they would take it to the Brewers Arms. When they put it inside the cage with the buck, he nearly killed it. He cut the flesh and fur off it, he would have killed my poor old rabbit if they hadn't taken it out. Blinking old Jim Hood had sold me a buck, not a doe, but I didn't keep them any more after Stanley Gifford gave me my first greyhound.

In the summer evenings I used to plait straw - sometimes as many as nine or even eleven straws at a time. The wheat straw was long then, and then I'd sew them round and make straw hats. You never see that done now - people don't have the time.

I was a bit handy with needlework. Before I was 12 years old I knitted myself a pair of gloves with some khaki wool and I put fur backs on them, so when I put my hands on the handlebars they didn't make my hands so cold. I also knitted myself a balaclava out of some old wool I had given me and it just had my face coming out, so I didn't get my ears cold. Then I knitted a navy blue hug-me-tight, which was in plain knitting and I used to wear it in school. It used to go right round me and kept me warm. It was like a cardigan, a tight fitting cardigan, with buttons down the front.

All the men on the farm used to keep their money in a Long Melford. That's a long, thin money bag. Charlie Bullock had one and that was wearing out. He was so good to me with my greyhounds so I thought 'I'll make Charlie Bullock a Long Melford'. Mother found me some chamois leather like they used to have them in. I cut it out wide enough to get your hand inside and long enough so that had two folds and stitched the side and bottom up. That's how they were made. If you were running

Skating party with the Old Man on the left and Tonardo Smith and myself on the right with Tickles

82

out of cash they'd say 'when its low tide at Harwich you've got to go to Long Melford'.

As soon as the ice froze over the old man would be looking to go skating. We all did. We had been building up to it and waiting for it, so as soon as the ice was strong enough, we'd tell everyone we could that we were going to have a skating party. We used to go down the lane and to the Skating Field, where the Bull pokers grow in the Summer, and the wild duck used to go. It was not too deep so we used to dare to skate on there when it would hardly bear us. When the weather got more frosty and the ice got so it could bear more we used to go to Newton Green pond or Mr Bean's pond at Levenheath. I've also skated on the pond at Cox Farm which the Kemball family had, but at Flatford mill hundreds of people would go when they flooded the meadow over the bridge. The Beans had a big pond, but they didn't skate themselves. Bert Cook would come so would Dick Rainham, The Dawsons, who were the clockmakers in Boxford, and the Steward girls. The Stewards came from the farm just before you get to the right hand side on the back road, before you get to the Sudbury turn, past Newton Green. Arthur Riddlesdell and his son Mark used to come - they kept the Boxford Post Office. Dad was the best skater by far, he was as good on the outside edge as he was on the inside edge and he could do a figure of eight or anything you asked him to do on one foot. He could do a three turn. He was a fancy skater. I had a pair of wooden skates. They were wooden with a steel blade in. You would screw them into the heel of your boot and then strap them round the toe. They took me over to Mr Bean's one day and to learn I had a chair and I would push behind the chair across the ice and that is the best way to learn. That's how Dad taught me and I've taught lots that way. We'd go at night time and have parties and people would get their cars round and put the head lights on so we could skate by car light and we'd take hot soup down there in flasks and also have hip flasks. At one of these skating parties at Newton Green I got my leg ripped and its bound up in the photo. Sid Rainham had struck out to skate off and he hit my leg and tore it. Tonardo Smith would come and skate and he took one of the pictures with my little camera - he's on the other one next to me and Tickles. I remember one night when we were skating down the lane someone said: "Look up there, look" and there was an old hare, he'd come up ever so close 'cause he'd heard all this noise going on and he was sitting there watching us all with his ears pricked in the moonlight.

WARD & SON LTD.
FAMOUS
GOLD MEDAL
ALES & STOUT

BREWERS, WINE & SPIRIT MERCHANTS

WARD & SON LTD

RECORDS OF   THE PAST

TRADE MARK

BREWERY FOXEARTH, ESSEX
Telephone No.10, Long Melford. Railway Station, Long Melford, 2½ Miles.

The old man said that Wards brewed the best beer in England, and so they did, they won more gold prizes than Guinness

Ru, Dad, Claude, Tickles and Edna
'Tom Clark let us have one of his punts on the river at Bures for the afternoon.'

Chapter 7

It's a fine summer's day and as balmy as May
With hounds to the village we'll come.
Every friend will be there and all trouble and care
Will be left far behind us at home.
See servants and steeds on their way
As sportsmen their garlands display
For we'll join the glad throng that goes laughing along
And we'll all go a hunting today
Then we'll a go a hunting to-day all nature is smiling an gay
For we'll join the glad throng that goes laughing along
And we'll all go a hunting today

Dad used to sing this, it has lots of verses

I wanted to learn to ride. I'd always promised myself I'd learn to ride as soon as we'd moved back to Red House Farm. It was on a Good Friday that we got the old grey mare out and I mounted her from the Josen Block. The Josen Block was the name of the mounting block in the farmyard and was there handy so that you could go up two or three steps and get on your horse on your own. Otherwise, someone would have to give you a leg up. I have been told that that's an ancient word that comes from jousting. Lazzie Pattle fixed me up with a saddle and stirrups and one thing and another and he ran up and down the road beside me, taught me to bump the saddle and that like, then the old man took me out after that with him on the old grey mare. She was quiet, but stood 15.2h. When it rained she hated it and would put her head right down between her front legs when she was trotting, she just couldn't stand the rain on her head. Then almost straight way I had to ride her to school and I had to stand her in the White Hart yard at Hadleigh at first. She'd stand there on pillar reins all day. That's with her back to the manger and a rein on either side of the bit to the next horse. I used to have to pay the ostler at The White Hart three pence a day for this. Later I took my pony to Billy Emeney. Billy Emeney was a jobmaster who hires out horses. Dad said: "I'll see him at Hadleigh market and arrange for you to put your pony in one of his boxes while you are at school.

The first time I went hunting, my father took me and the hounds met at Boxford. We went up to Bulls Cross Wood I was eight or nine and there was a little jump - a ditch. My father had me on a lead rope. We went over this little jump and he says to me: "Don't sit so far back, sit a little forwarder." So I was leaning forward and the mare jumped and I went over her head. So I picked myself up and got on again and he said: "Let's have another go, don't sit so far forward this time." So I sat further back and when the old mare went over the jump I fell off over the tail. I didn't want to go over no more jumps that day but he made me - until I could sit on.

The Pattle's were horse dealers, they were from Bakers Green, Boxford. Old Bill Pattle was the father and he had several sons and I knew them all well. Daniel Pattle, he was the eldest one. The next one to him was Lazzie, he'd got two or three children and his wife ran away and left him. He worked for my father then while we lived at Sampson Hall and when his little girl was about seven or eight he went down to Hadleigh and bought her a new jersey, a red one. He lived at Groton wood near where the Master of the Hounds built his house, and when he went home, this little girl - she'd got lovely black curly hair she wanted to see how she looked in the jersey. She stood up in front of the

Lazzie Pattle talking to Dad

overmantle mirror over the fire and the flames came out and caught her dress and burnt her, burnt her to death. That was on the Saturday night and on the Sunday morning, ever so early, mother came up to my bedroom and said: "Ru, I want your night-dress". We had all put our clean night-dresses on Saturday night, she said "I want your clean night-dress", (the one I was sleeping in) "Lazzie Pattle's little girl's been burnt, and he hasn't got a night-dress to put her in to take her to hospital." I took off my night-dress and that's where it went. She never came out of the hospital and that broke his heart, poor old Lazzie. He always seemed to take an interest in me. He was a wise old boy with horses and the old ways. His family had been dealing in horses for years and he told me lots of things.

Lazzie had a son named Golden who worked at Red House farm as well. Lazzie also had a brother called Golden, and another called Oaty. Golden the younger brother was stone deaf. Oaty used to work on the farm at times. They lived in a Caravan as boys. They'd go to Ireland with their father Bill and buy a drove of horses and bring them back to this country. They'd sell some of them when they got off the boat and they'd gradually bring them home and they'd sell a few here and there as they drove them all the way across the country. There'd be twenty or thirty of these horses in a drove, and old Mr Tapper used to have his stick and somebody would come along and say: "See that brown hoss there, I'd like to see 'im" and the sons they'd single it out the drove and they used to run and jump on it bare back and give him a gallop while it was in the drove. When old man Bill Pattle was at Boxford, he

Reprint from Sudbury Free Press

100 years ago 1905

WILLIAM Pattle, horse dealer, Boxford, was brought up on a charge of having been drunk while in charge of a horse and cart on the previous night in King Street, Sudbury.

Inspector Reeve stated that at half-past 11, as he was leaving the police station he saw a horse and cart standing in front of the Bear Hotel.

On going to the cart, however, he found Pattle lying athwart the front part, his legs being in front of one wheel and his head towards the other. He was in a perfectly helpless condition of drunkenness.

The defendant refused to be taken home so the inspector had to lock him up for his own safety.

Pattle said he was drinking with "a gentleman" and that at 75 years of age he couldn't stand the drink as he used to. He was sorry and said he had never been up in front of magistrates before.

Inspector Reeve asked for the expense of putting up the horse; he had to call the landlord of the public house up to get the horse stabled.

Pattle was fined 18s, which he was easily able to do out of the £83 in gold found on him. He seemed to be gratified that the police had taken care of him and his money, though he thought the bed at the police station was rather hard.

lived in this caravan and he got a bootmaker to make him boots because his feet were so big. So the bootmaker made some boots - buttonsided boots and he took them up for him to try them on at the caravan. He asked how much they were and the man told him, but when he tried them on he said they were too tight.

He'd tried them on and old Bill said: "Oh dear, Oh dear, Oh dear, they are much too tight, much too tight, they are no good to me they are too tight". The man said: "I can't take them back Mr Pattle, I made them especially for you. No one else will have them. No one else has feet that big". The man wanted his money. He said: "Look Mr Pattle if I charge you so much for 'em," which was about half the price, "would you have them then?".

Old Pattle said: "Now your talkin'. You see they didn't fit him when they were £1, but they'd fit him all right at ten shillings". None of 'em could read or write - they didn't need to. One day when old Pattle was waiting for the train he made out he was reading a paper when somebody passing by said, "Bill, you've got your newspaper upside down", Bill replied: "Any dang fool can read it the other way up".

They used to call Lassie, Decon, that was his nick-name. He taught me to ride on a Good Friday. He put me up on a horse.

My father asked him, when he was paying him one day: "Shall I pay you this way or that way, Lazzie which would you prefer?" Lazzie said: "Well Gov'nor you know me I've never preferred in my life".

Mother used to make Lazzie a Christmas pudding every year and on Christmas morning we'd all walk over with it to his home by Groton wood. He was a wise old man and people used to come miles to see him and ask him questions about horses and such like. In the 1920s when there was an outbreak of foot and mouth disease Lazzie just said 'treat 'em with Stockholm Tar and Salt and they'll get better' and so they did. He so loved nature and knew all about it - the weather and the seasons.

They had some rum old names in those days. There was one old boy called Vinegar. He came off the dole. He was one of those that didn't want to work, he would rather have been left on the dole. Anyway during the depression they sent him up to work up on a farm and his wages were six pence an hour. I felt sorry for him. I used to make some wine in those days. I was talking about the wine I made and he said he'd like to try it. Some I'd made was so sour, it was like vinegar we couldn't drink it. He said that didn't matter and he would still like to try it. So I took him a bottle and it wasn't sweet enough but he drank it and that was like vinegar and ever after then we called him Vinegar.

There was another old boy called Dakka Wright. He was born called Dakka. He was Mr Kemball's gamekeeper up at Cox Farm. His boy was working at the farm up the road and he's called Dakka.

Everybody had horses years ago. You had to afore engines came in. Horses were your transport. They were your power to cultivate the land as well. If you did not know about horses you'd get your leg lifted. You had to know about horses, their good points and bad, to survive. They were never a plaything.

My Father always had horses. He loved horses as his father had done. We had a drove of young blood horses. We had three brood mares - Marchinelle, she was a chestnut, Chantillie was the name of the grey one, because she was by a horse called Le Samay. She had Samay blood in her, (he was a famous race horse in France). I've forgotten what the other one was. Dad had bred them, but I think he bought Marchinelle. We used to breed from these regularly. One day Godbold the vet came over from Sudbury to castrate one or two young horses. By the back door to the left, past the apple tree, was a pear tree and beyond that was another tree and beyond that was a yellow plum tree and it happened under that yellow plum tree. They brought the colts out. Godbold wanted to throw it over on the ground by tying it's leg up, the old man said that he didn't like that, but the vet said he was the professional and that was the way he always did it (I suppose he was scared of getting kicked by doing it standing up as most people did). We all went into the house and the next thing was Godbold knocked on the door for a gun, he said: "I've just broken his leg" and that was the end of him. I can remember him, he just had a dab of white across his nose, he was a bay, a lovely colt. Dad was so upset. He had ordered all us children indoor 'cause Godbold had come to castrate these horses and we weren't allowed to be anywhere near that. After that he had the vet from Kersey, Donald Lemon.

The daughter of Marchinelle was a chestnut mare and we used her for breeding. The army commandeered five horses for the First World War, took them at £55 a piece and we thought that was a lot of money then but horses made a lot more money after the war. They just came and took your horses you know. I can remember them taking a horse named Tango, a chestnut with white legs and another one we called Bent Legs, 'cause that was a little bit bent at the front and the old man had to plead with them to leave the chestnut mare so he'd got something to breed from. He said: "I shan't be able to breed no more horses if you take her away" This mare, Marchinelle, had lots of foals. We still kept breeding what we could even through the bad years selling some here and there. Dad loved horses, but then his father did, he was bred to 'em - we always had horses. He had some beautiful horses then and most had foals.

I went on a meet on my own one day. I rode Vixen, the mare that I bought off Stanley Gifford when I was 13. The old mare was a good jumper. I think the meet was at Hintlesham Hall. From Hintlesham Hall we went in all those woods round about there and then they found a fox and they went away, I don't know what country they went through, but they went through very pretty country, with a lot of gorse about on barren lands. I remember being on top of that and looking over to Mistley and

Manningtree. When we were on the way there I was cantering my old mare and we were cantering on the grass, because you mustn't canter a horse on the hard road, I either passed, or was in front of, the man who reported for the East Anglian Daily Times. He was a wealthy plumber in Ipswich and he also wrote pieces for the paper, and he wrote a piece for the East Anglian saying 'When I was going towards Mistley, the little girl on the chestnut mare fairly got the legs of me, I was thinking of the morrow and she was out for the day.' I was no age at all then, about 12.

Stanley Gifford would do anything for a wager. He had galloped this poor old mare, Vixen, from Stoke Crown down to Nayland which is more than a mile and on the hard road to beat Fred Kingsbury's car for a bet. Dad wanted a horse for Edna. I was then showing horses for a Mr Partridge who was a dealer at Wetherden Maypole. He had a horse called Swannee who was

nappy and wouldn't go for everyone but I got on well with her. I just kept talking to her. But if you had a whip and touched her she'd lay her ears and nap it. She could not be moved then. I told Dad about her and he swapped her for an unbroken mare. Dad didn't know at the time that Swannee had been 'broken down' - she had a big tendon, but she'd got over it and apart from that she was sound.

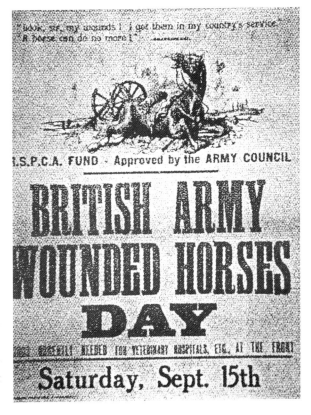

"Look, sir, my wounds! I got them in my country's service. A horse can do no more!"

I.S.P.C.A. FUND - Approved by the ARMY COUNCIL

BRITISH ARMY WOUNDED HORSES DAY

MONEY NEEDED FOR VETERINARY HOSPITALS, ETC., AT THE FRONT

Saturday, Sept. 15th

Dad's horse in those days was Sparks and he also had been discharged out the army and had the discharge mark on him in the same way as Vixen. After the 1914-1918 war the Pattle's would go down to Colchester and come back with a drove of horses that had come back from the war.

They say that two and a half million horses went to that terrible war and less than one in a hundred came back.

The RSPCA had a special day to beg anyone with any veterinary know - how to go out there because it was carnage. These poor old things were being strapped up to gun carriages and the like and being flogged through the mud and sludder and then blown to bits by shells. One day Bill Pattle and his boys drove some of these horses into the yard. Dad asked about one with something funny in his eye. He was walking lame too. Dad said: "What's up with that horse Bill? I reckon he's lost an eye in the Dardanelles 'Yes' said bill 'and in Boxford lost a shoe'. He was as poor as a crow when Dad bought him. He was his favourite horse. Stanley Gifford borrowed him not long after Dad got him round to try him out and took him jumping at the show at West Bergholt. Coming back he went over a part of the farm called the Queech which is at the bottom of Race Course field. It is a great big ditch and it always had water in the bottom and he jumped right up and out the other side and when he told Dad he didn't believe him. They all went down and had a look and they could see the marks where he had done it so Dad knew that Sparks could jump.

The old man on Sparks - his favourite horse. He came back from the 14-18 war with a discharge brand on him

One day we got the horses out to ride. Dad rode Sparks and Edna rode Vixen because she thought she could hold Vixen better and Dad didn't want her to ride the new horse in case it had any pranks; so I rode the new horse, Swannee. When we got into the bottom of Gypps Piece field we were going to turn and walk up the field, but when we turned their heads, all of a sudden, the old chestnut mare, Vixen, shot off, because that is how they would start races and I suppose she thought she was in a race. She went right up the top of the field, damn near half a mile with Edna sitting on the back. It was no good me galloping after her because she'd only have gone gone faster. She galloped up the field, right along the brew and there was a gateway in the corner. As she galloped up the fence Vixen threw Edna off and then galloped off home into her box. It's a good job she did. That taught me to shut the stable door top and bottom every time you take a horse out. Edna never rode again.

I was about 15 then and I thought I'd have Swannee 'cause she was a younger horse and sell the old mare. So I then advertised Vixen for sale. A man replied that he was coming up by train to see her. I had to meet him at Sudbury station, I had to hack the old mare 8 miles to Sudbury station. When I got there the man looked at her and then asked if he could ride her. He got on her and went round the corner and he was gone, and he was gone ages. I did not know whether to

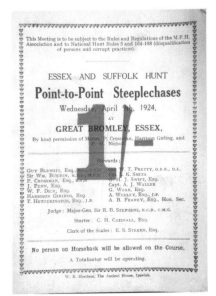

2.45 **The Farmers' Race.** (*Entrance Free*)

A Cup, presented by Percy Crossman, Esq., M.F.H. Second 5 sovs. For maiden horses (point-to-point races only excepted) that have been regularly and fairly hunted with the Essex and Suffolk Hounds, season 1923-4. The property of bona-fide farmers occupying land within the limits of the Essex and Suffolk Hunt. To be ridden by a farmer occupying land within the limits of the Essex and Suffolk Hunt, or by a subscriber to the Essex and Suffolk Hunt. Weights, 12st. 7lbs., or over. Not less than three miles of fair hunting country. Post entries. The winner of a race in 1924 7lbs. extra, of two or more 10lbs.

1 Mr. C. H. Chisnall's bay m , **Abbess**, aged.
2 Mr. Bob Chilver's bay g., **Whisky**, aged.
3 Mr. D. C. Gales' bay g., **Sweet Boy**, aged.
4 Mr. Harrison Girling's blk. m., **Shady Lady**, aged.
5 Mr. A. S. R. Cooper's ch. g., **Roger**, 5 years.
6 Mr. F. A. Girling's bay g., **Branbags**, aged.
7 Mr. George Wade's ch. g., **Bombadier**, aged.
8 Miss Ruby Alliston's br. m., **Swanee**, aged.
9 Mr. W. A. Mudd's br. m , **Primrose**, aged.
10 Mr. George Cooper's bay m., **Trini**, aged.
11 Mr. R. E. Giles' bay m., **Kitty**, aged.
12 Mr. H. C. Raynham's bay m., **Utility**, 5 years.

cry or what to do. I thought I've lost my horse. I knew if I told my father he would say: "You bloody fool", he would have called me everything. Last of all this man brought the mare back, brought the old girl back to me. I thought now I've got to get on her and hack her back to Boxford. When he brought her back I said: "Where ever have you been?" He said: "I've just galloped her up Ballingdon Hill to see if her wind was all right" Ballingdon Hill was miles away, right on the other side of Sudbury. In the end he bought her for £23.00. so I then bought Swannee off the Old Man for £24.00. which I thought was a good deal.

Swanee was my horse and I hunted her and rode her everywhere, but she would sometimes nap. She was a full blooded horse, could stay and had speed and was game, but if you hit her or she didn't like anything she'd stop dead and no power on earth could move her. I thought I would get her fit for the point to point season but Dad would not let me ride her so I

In my riding habit on Swannee the nappy mare

got Cyril Boreham to ride her. Cyril and his brother Ben were the best point to point riders and they were friends of Dad.

Cyril Boreham, he was the best point-to-point rider of his day

I told Cyril Boreham what she was like and he promised me not to touch her and I asked him again at the start of the race, but he knew too much and he just had to drop her one down the shoulder at the start of the race. So there she stood, she stuck her toes in the ground and wouldn't move. He couldn't make her move and he realised what he'd done. Like everybody else, he didn't think I knew what I was talking about. After a little while she walked off, then she got into a trot, then she got into a canter and by the time the other horses had got half way round she'd overhauled them. At half way round she was there, at three quarters of the way round she was leading by a field. She was beating an exceptionally good mare, I don't remember what she was called. It was down hill to the last jump and then you jumped over a fence and went uphill. Of course Cyril Boreham leading all this long way cantered her down and couldn't resist giving her another one. She landed on the other side of the jump, and when she landed on the other side she stuck her toes in again, she wouldn't go. He had to try and persuade her to go, he eventually got her to walk off, and she walked past the winning post and was just beaten by about a length by the other horse. She walked past the winning post - bloody idiot wasn't he. I could do anything with her though.

When I had Vixen, each year the Hunter Improvement Society used to send a stallion round. It cost a pound to farmers to cross breed a mare. The next year Vixen had a foal I called her Tishy she was by Roeshetto. The mare had lost her milk when she was three days old and the poor little thing was starving. We didn't know what to do for milk because they need their beestings - the first milk - but I bought it up on Quaker Oats. I used to take them to her in a little tin, and she'd put her nose in and eat that. Nowadays you can buy the milk to give to a foal. When she was about three years old she used to be turned out with the other horses. The cowman, however, made a mistake and put the bull in the same field. When the cows went out, the bull went with them. This bull hated horses. He gored my poor little Tishy and penetrated it. If it had been a flesh wound it would have been all right but it went through her ribs. Dad had gone down the lane to look at the horses and this little horse came up to him and kept rubbing on him and as he patted her, he saw the wound. We took her home and put her in the bottom stable, with the double doors. Tishy leant on the door and died leaning on it with her head over that half-door whinnying for me but I could do nothing for her. That upset me terribly.

We had one before that, a brown filly and that died when I was on holiday with the family at Walton. Something went wrong with it 'cause when I got back my Father said the foal was dead. I sold Vixen after that. She was getting on a bit. Once she ran away with me when I was coming home from Hadleigh. I couldn't hold one side of her and luckily enough the gate to the farmyard was closed so she stopped and put her head over the top of that. She was a full blood horse and had been raced. As soon as you were with two more horses on either side she wanted to go. If anything came up beside her she used to go like hulloo-ya.

Tickles on Tishy, which was shortly afterwards gored to death by the bull, Ru and greyhounds

That rotten old bull had already got out one day in the front meadow. The cows were in the back meadow and Swannee was in the front meadow. He went for Swannee, he put his head down and went for her and got her underneath the chest lifted her off the ground and flung her about, but she got up and away so Harry Tricker said, 'cause he saw it happen.

Tishy as a yearling

One day Dad said: "Get on that old mare Ru". Well she was 14 years old and unbroken. You can't start riding horses unbroken at that age, but he made me get on. Dad never cared what he put me on - he'd put me on anything. When I rode the mare I couldn't hold one side of her, she just used to go. She was a nasty mare and a lot of trouble - the same one that cut her head open. I got the saddle on her. I don't know how I got on, but I went down to seven acres, Dad came down and said: "Now canter her across seven acres"; she had never been broken. I cantered down seven acres; of course I had a job to hold her, you can imagine, she was a wild thing. After that I remember going back to take her home and put her in the stable. I never rode her any more. It's no good breaking a horse in at 14 years old.

We had a very nice Shire mare. She had a foal and we sent her to Sudbury show - Wickhambrook Colt Show - that was held at People Park, Sudbury. It was such a hot day, the sun scorched overhead and the horses had no shelter, there was not a tree anywhere. The mare came in first and when they went to trot her out she couldn't trot, she couldn't move, she was paralysed by the sun. They managed to get her into the float and got her home. They put her out on the meadow and she laid down and never got up no more, she died there and left the foal. The foal was alright and we called it Scot. Her mother was a quiet mare a right good looker, she wasn't anymore than 5 years old. We then brought the foal up.

Nabs was my last horse and my favourite. I bred her from that chestnut mare that the old man made me ride when she was fourteen years old. Her sire was a Premium Stallion called Lord Hillary. They were subsidised by the Hunter Improvement Society, so the stud fee was only a pound. The mare was turned out at Hadleigh, 5 miles away. We had to go over and see how she was - Dad didn't even know the time she should foal. I went over one time and she had foaled. I said I'll take her home. We got a bullock float to get the foal in and went over with a horse to pull it. I don't know how ever we managed but we got the foal inside the float. Once that was inside the float, the mare walked behind. A man came with me. He led the horse that was in the shafts of the float and I stood in there - in the float with the foal and held it so it couldn't jump out. It had a little headcollar on and I held it and kept patting it. That stood on my feet so many times, it made my feet blue, but I held it 'till I got home. Why I went to all this trouble was because my father had promised it to me in place of Tishy my little horse the bull had gored, so it was mine by rights. It was a rare pretty little foal with no white on it. When it was about two months old, somebody from Newmarket advertised for a foal, must be a whole colour - no white on it - a thoroughbred foal. What they were going to do with it I can't think but we reckoned that somebody in Newmarket had had a valuable foal that had died and they were going to put that in place of it. A man named Clark from Hundon came to have a look

I Charles Alleston do give my daughter Ruby the Chestnut Imare's foal by Lord Hillary.

x Signed. Charles Alleston.
1928 June 22nd With Love

Witness Phyllis Girling

at it, but it wasn't any good, there was something a little bit different about my foal. Dad had given me this foal, and I had brought it home and then, when there was chance he thought he was going to make some money out of it, he offered it for sale to the people who wanted to replace their foal. That annoyed me intensely. It was in the top meadow and it was about then that all the men on the farm started having Saturday afternoon off. The mare and foal on the top meadow hadn't got any water. Water had to be carted in pails from the pond in the farmyard all the way up to the top meadow. Dad said: "You cart some water up Ruby". I was so savage to think he'd given me the foal and then offered it to someone else, I said: "Yesterday it was your horse, you cart it up your bloody self, I'm not going to water your horse". He said: "Yes, well it is your horse, I never sold it, I only showed it to them," and he made a lot of excuses. I went and I carted the water, two pails at a time. I said: "Before I do it

The old man with the foal that lost its mother through sun stroke at the South Suffolk Show in People's Park, Sudbury

you write in black and white that it's mine", which he did and Phyllis our mothers help witnessed it.

In those days I was sought after to ride in the ladies' competitions. Bill Partridge, who kept Wetherden Maypole, had got a very nice horse and he asked me to ride it. Also there was a girl named Mary Makin, who lived in Hadleigh, whose father was a Job master. She used to do a bit of riding for him but I was to ride it at the Bromley horseshow. When the day came I had to be there in good time because of the judging. I asked my father

if he was going and he said he didn't think so. He said: "If you want to go, you'll have to ride the motorbike." But he knew that the motorbike wasn't working properly and was unreliable. I started out and I got as far as Ardleigh Lion then it conked out, so I put it in Ardleigh Lion yard and I walked out onto the road and stood in the road hoping I could get a lift. Along came Charlie Rainham in his horse and trap, he said: "What are you doing here Ru?" I said: "My motorbike's broken down". He said: "Jump in I'll take you". So I went to the show and I wasn't worrying about how I was going to get home. I rode this horse in the ladies' class and I won; then I rode it for the Championship of the Show and I won the

102

Best Ladies' Hunter and Bill Partridge sold it there and then to a man named Tom Howard. He made a lot of money out of it. Bill Partridge never told me that the horse had run away. Apparently this girl Mary Maken from Hadleigh had ridden it and it ran away with her. It wanted a very strong armed person to hold it. Partridge kept saying to me: "When you go round the narrow part at the bottom of the ring, hold him in tight, let him out on the straight so they can see how well he can gallop, but be ever so careful round the narrow part of the ring". I didn't know why, but I rode him according to his instructions. I was strong in the arm. I apparently rode it well and he was very pleased. As I came out of the ring somebody nipped up beside of me and said: "Well done Ru, well done Ru". It was my Father, he'd gone to the show after all. He said: "When you put the horse away, I'll take you in to have some tea". I said: "No thank you". I was cross with Dad to think he'd let me struggle to get to the show on that useless motorbike. I needed to look smart in that ring, you can't be clean when you are riding a motorbike, all the dust goes on your jodhpurs and everywhere.

Nip was the fox terrier that Freddy Theobald gave us. He always used to come in the stable when I was grooming Nabs, and I used to put him in the manger. I'd give Nip Nab's lead to hold and he'd lead her out of the box. He'd sit on the saddle as well and hold the reins as if he were riding her. He loved it did little Nip.

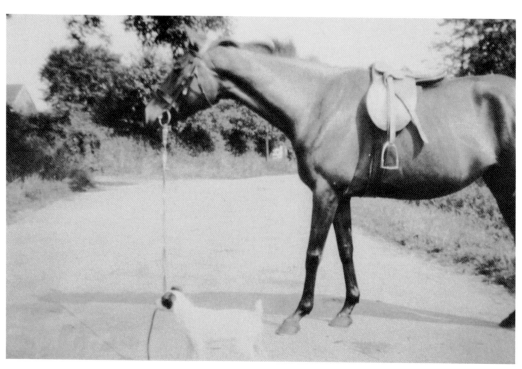

Nabs with Nip the dog given to me by Freddy Theobald. Freddy was later killed by a bus in Melford Street

Chapter 8

The Jolly Waggoner

When I first went a-waggoning
A-waggoning did go
I filled my parent's hearts with grief
Full of sorrow, care and woe
And many were the hardships
That I did undergo
Sing whoa my lads, sing whoa
Drive on my lads i.o
Who would not lead the stirring life we jolly waggoners do.

T'was on a dark and stormy night
When wetted to the skin
We bare it with a contented heart
Until we reached the Inn
And there we'll sit about the fire
With the landlord and his kin
Sing whoa my lads, sing whoa
Drive on my lads i.o
Who would not lead the stirring life we jolly waggoners do.

When Michaelmas has come at last
What pleasure we shall find
We'll make the gold to fly boys
Like chaff before the wind
And every lad will take his lass
To sit upon his knee
Sing whoa my lads, sing whoa
Drive on my lads i.o
Who would not lead the stirring life we jolly waggoners do.

I have no idea who I learned this from but the old
horsemen used to sing it

One day a fox went to ground near our wood. It went to ground
in a ditch. An old man named Surridge, a rotten old devil who
lived in the tin bungalow at the end of Justice Wood, came down
and said: "Dig it out and kill it" I said: "No you don't. If it's gone

to ground, you leave it for another day". Anyway he got to arguing with Dad and they eventually left it in as it happened to be in our side of the fence. If it had been the other side it would have been dug out and killed by old Surridge. The hounds then went off to find another fox and they drew Justice Wood but my Father left a man there, standing in his field, by where the fox had gone in. If not old Surridge would have come on our land and dug it out and killed it. Once they ran a fox down into Twenty Acre Husks and the fox went to ground in a ditch and they were going to dig him out there, but before the old man could get there and say anything, they'd killed it. I was coming on after and I was presented with the brush by the Master, Sir William Burton. I had one or two foxes' brushes presented to me but I never had a mask. I didn't use to want them, I could not bear the fox being killed. I just loved the sport of riding. I have come to the conclusion that just as much pleasure can be had having a drag hunt.

When I was about 14 and I still hadn't got a saddle of my own, I had to use my Father's. I saved up, I had £4 and I went to Ipswich and bought a saddle in the auction. I used to go up to the market at Spurling and Hempson and also Bonds, they were the auctioneers. The old man would send some cows up, when he wanted some money. He'd say: "Ru, they've got to make so much money" and I used to have to go up there (sometimes,

Bond's auction Ipswich

even drive them all the way and walk behind) and then sort out the dealers and take them to look at the cows. The one I got the best offer off, I sold afterwards 'cause they'd often be unsold in the auction.

Baker, the drover from Hadleigh, always waved and said hello if I saw him on the road. He was a tall, good-looking young man and drove cattle along the

roads for a living. I've often driven cattle into Ipswich market. Walked every step. If you had two or three heifers that you wanted to sell - that was the only way.

When I wanted a hunting coat, Mother bought the material and they made me a coat, and they made the breeches. They took Dad's breeches for a pattern and I had buck skin strapping and they were quite nice for a little girl. As I grew older I had two more riding coats made for me in Hadleigh by Mr Kettle the Tailor. They were always long, flared coats and when I sat on the horse it dropped down at the sides. They were called riding habits. During that time I had a pair of corduroy breeches. I also had a pair that matched the coat and I had another pair, a sort of sandy colour but they were proper jodhpurs. These coats were made of dark grey worsted. They had a high waist and were long, nearly down to the knee. They wore them like that in those days. Now they wear short coats. I had a hard hat that was my Father's - a bowler hat - and I had a pig tail hanging down the back. Tickles wore a hard hat with a peak when he hunted.

People that rode hunting had top hats. They had to pay a subscription, but the farmers didn't pay a subscription and to wear a peaked cap was known 'the farmers privilege'. Farmers used to walk foxhound puppies. Jack Dakin always had a couple, he farmed at Sherbourne House Farm, Edwardstone. There were three of them. There was Jack and another brother and a sister, none of them married. Jack Dakin used to sit next to my Father in Sudbury Grammar school. Reggie Dyer used to sit the other side. He had a farm at Boxford. He sat between them at school, then he farmed between them after he left. Jack Dakin was a big farmer, he used to farm at Polstead Ponds. They sold that and went to live at Sherbourne House. That's when Peter Nott had Polstead Ponds Farm. I've been down to Polstead Ponds times, sometimes with my Father, as I got older on my bicycle and then I used to walk across the meadow to where Maria Marten was murdered. She was murdered at the Red Barn. The footings of the Red Barn were still there. People used to go there and take a brick or two away, so I think it's nearly gone now. Polstead Park had a lot of deer in it. It was famous because it had the remainder of an oak tree, which although it was still green was split down the middle but there was still a portion of it there. On a certain Sunday every year they hold a church service underneath that tree. They did that because that's where they said the gospel was first preached in East Anglia. In the church yard there was a stone that was put up to Maria Marten. People that went to see it used to chip a bit off to take it away until it got so small, it wasn't no bigger than a football and they took it into the church then, so people shouldn't interfere with it.

Frank Boreham was the son of Billy Boreham and old Billy Boreham lived at Langham Mill. He used to break horses and we would pay him - that was his living. He used to have this great big thing that they used to break horses in and they used to sit up ever so high when they used to drive them beside another one. There was a pole up the middle of the doings. They used to put another horse on, a steady old horse. When they broke them into harness, they would put the colt or the young horse in beside it and drive them. Frank was a great friend of Dad's when he was young. Frank Boreham was a beggar, he was a daredevil, he would do any damn thing. They used to get so tight they didn't know what they were doing. Frank's father lived at Nayland Mill and he used to go from Langham down to Stratford St Mary and get tight. Then they'd put him in the bottom of the cart and the old pony would take him home - he knew his way home. Then they used to take the pony out of the harness, let the shafts go up and shoot him out the back. They used to get up to all sorts of larks and wagers. They used to put so much in the hat and the landlord at The Crown at Stoke by Nayland used to hold the money. They used to ride over the fields, alongside the road from Stoke Crown to Thorington Street Barn, touch Thorington Street Barn and come back and who ever got back first took the money. One day, Frank Boreham had got a very nice little horse, which he had won a point to point or two with, it was called Buxom. He rode this little horse at this fence - a stiff holly hedge, wide across the top, that must have been six foot high, that was round The Crown yard and he jumped it, but I think he came down. When he jumped it he

Honor Bright

landed in The Crown yard. Of course he never should have put his horse at that fence. It jumped it but it was never any good any more. I don't know what happened, but it was never any more good.

One day there was a lot of them in the Fleece at Boxford and they went out in the yard to race - to run round the yard. There was Bumper Kemble, Dad, Frank Boreham running against Peter Towns. He was a great big man and he came from out Levenheath somewhere; he was a farmer. As he was running someone stuck their foot out and Peter Towns fell down and they had a rare job to get him in the cart to get him home. He wasn't any more good either, he was a gonna, he fell on his big stomach. They never knew who did it but it wasn't the done thing and there'd have been hell to pay if they'd found out who it was.

Old Billy Boreham lived at Langham Mill and also his son was Frank Boreham who Dad was friendly with as a young man. He was always doing daredevil things. He had two sons, Cyril and Ben. He was the one with the horse breaking machine. Ben was at Framlingham college at school. Cyril moved from Langham to take Edwardstone Park Farm where he went in partnership with George Wade. Ben used to write to me from Framlingham and Mother one day opened my letter, I was annoyed about that. I wasn't very pleased about that because he was only a boy at school. When he left school he went down to Newmarket to be

Cyril and Ben Boreham, their mother and father Frank at Williams Farm, Thorington Street

an apprentice jockey. Ben used to ride Lively when he was just a boy. Ben's wife was Betty Boreham and she used to train greyhounds for a man called Coulson who was a bookmaker in Colchester. He also had a horse in training which won a big race (the Cambridgeshire or something like that). They did not have greyhound racing then, it was all coursing meetings and there was always bookmakers there to take the bets.

Stanley Gifford's mother was a good horsewoman. She had a horse named Roxanna, she used to hunt. One day she jumped Dedham lock, side saddle. You know what a lock is like, there is no take off and there is no landing. You either jump it or go right in. One slip and you're a gonna. That's sheer take off and sheer landing. She jumped it for a wager.

Mr. Jorrocks counts twenty.

The Giffords were running out of money. Old Mr Gifford could not afford a good hunter for his wife anymore. One day she mounted on a barge horse and rode it into the bar of the Marlborough Pub at Dedham, where he was, to show him up. She was a character. Stanley had her horse Roxanna for years and years, she had a lot of foals.

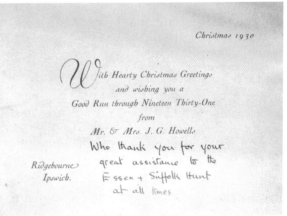

The old man went down to Dedham with a young horse, a three year old. That was a flea bitten grey but beautiful mare. It had just been broken. She was handy to ride but she was nervous like a young horse generally is. So they'd all had too much to drink and they come out the pub. The old man got his horse out and got the reins and got someone to give him a leg up. Instead of giving him a leg up into the saddle, they give him a leg up behind the saddle. Of course, the horse just bucked and bucked and flung the old man off and cut his eye open and banged his head. Then they put him on the horse and tied his legs underneath and he got home all right.

There was a Jobmaster in Ipswich named Arthur Cannon. A Jobmaster would buy horses and let them out for any purpose. He supplied horses to the Yeomanry when they were training.

He used to hire them from farmers and pay them so much for the use of their horse and my horse Swannee went down. I think I got £10 for the fortnight. Cannon was the same man that bought Lively, this little 14.2h mare. She was chestnut but a blood'un and a streak down her face. I rode her once or twice in the shows and she always won the hack class. She was bought out of the army. Cyril Boreham bought her for £24.00 off two brothers. Ben Boreham used to ride her and she used to win all the jumping competitions at the County Shows and Cyril used to say she always paid the rent on the farm. Cyril Boreham sent her up to Olympia, Ben rode her at the International Challenge Cup for jumping and won. Cyril said: "We'll fill that old cup up when she comes home". When she come home it was such a big cup that he couldn't afford to fill it and that little mare won it. When I rode it in the hack class, Cyril used to have a square cart there that the farmers used to go out on and he used to put her in the shafts to show her. He used to win that class as well - she won everything. She also had a 'S' on her shoulder where she had come out the army after the 1914-1918 war. That was called

The Essex and Suffolk Point to Point at Bromley 1924.
Photo courtesy of Miss Pat Freeman

a Utility Class when he drove her in the shafts. Then he'd take her out the shafts and I used to ride her in the Hack Class. This was at the Suffolk Show. Then after the Hack Class, she used to go in the jumping and she'd win that, all on the same day. She'd come home with a string of rosettes on her bridle from the Suffolk Show or wherever she went.

So I hired Swannee out for Yeomanry training. The Yeomanry spent a fortnight at Felixstowe. I was working at Felixstowe as a hairdresser and I went down to the camp. When I went to check that she was all right, I could not find her, so I got the Sergeant in Charge to walk down the line with me. All of a sudden I said: "There she is, look, that's her". He said: "That isn't her." I said: "That's her" He said: "That isn't her, she's unrideable. One of the Officers got on her this morning and tried to ride her and she wouldn't budge. We are putting her down in the morning, she is unrideable". I said: "That's my mare. I patted her on the neck, I said: "Have you got a saddle". I'd got a dress on mind you. He said: "I don't know what saddle we've got." He went and had a look, all he could find me was an old army saddle. So I said: "Pop

Ben Boreham on Lively - who won every class she could enter at the Suffolk show where I rode her

it on her back" He'd got a snaffle bridle on it, he gave me a leg up. All he could say was: "I wouldn't do that, I wouldn't do that, she'll kill yer" I said: "She'll never kill me". I cocked my leg over the back, patted her on the neck and she walked off as good as gold. The sergeant stood there and didn't know what to do. The guns that they'd got down there were pointing out to sea, there were three or four and I cantered her in and out of the guns and she went beautiful, lovely, never made any fuss, so I had her back. I think when they tried to ride her down there she put her stifle out.

When I was out with the hunt down at Stoney Down Wood one day I jumped

HAPPY CHRISTMAS & NEW YEAR
FROM
A. J. & V. MUNNINGS

CASTLE HOUSE,
DEDHAM,
COLCHESTER.

1957-58

A Christmas card from Sir Alfred Munnings when he mentioned me in his book

out of the Wood up into twenty acres. It was a little bit up hill and she fell. She fell into the next field, and she rolled over as she fell and she broke my hand. She got up and cantered off home, she knew where she was. I walked home with my hand blown up, there was nobody at home when I got there, so I got on my bike and went to Hadleigh to Dr Everett. He looked at my hand and he said: "There are so many little bones in your hand, I can't very well set it. So I just had it done up. I then advertised poor old Swannee and sold her.

One day the Eastern Counties Otter Hounds met at Boxford. I went down there and followed them on foot along the river all the way until I got to Higham. At Higham bridge I didn't go any further, I was whacked absolutely done up and luckily someone gave me a lift home to Boxford.   At Higham there lived an old boy called Freddy Boucher who'd got plenty of money, rich as a sheeny he was. It was left to him by an Aunt I think and he used to go down to Newmarket and buy up bloodstock. Anything he saw he liked, he bought. He used to take them home and train them on, more often than not he'd turn them out on the meadow and that's where they'd stop. Eventually he might sell one to a farmer for a trifle or give it to them. He used to hunt and he had a horse named Criptical. I once went to a point to point and Freddy Boucher had got three horses entered and all three of them won. I can't remember the name of the first horse, one of them was named Wellington, one was Criptical. Then Criptical went on and he ran Criptical at Liverpool in the Foxhunter Steeplechase and he won it. He was a great big bay horse with great big feet, it was over the Grand National course. A day or two after I saw him out hunting and I said: "Congratulations Mr Boucher". He said: "Oh, thank you very much" because Mr Boucher wasn't very popular with the hunt. They had a job to get his subscription out of him, but to me he was popular 'cause he had some very good horses. He used to ride very long - with long leathers. All his horses could jump. When I congratulated him he asked if I would like a photograph of Criptical. I said: "Yes please, I would", but I never got it. He was a real eccentric. If you went to see Mr Boucher for

Ben Portway, Kenya 1926

anything, if he asked you in you were lucky. He would sit on the settee and say: "Will you have a drink?" then he'd put his hand underneath the settee and pull out a bottle, generally port wine, and give you a drink. He spent untold money on horses, but nothing on himself. He always looked scruffy, his hunting coat was always a bit spotted. He had some horses in training in Newmarket. I think they were with Oates the trainer. When he went down to see the horses out, he often left Higham to go to Newmarket in his dressing gown. He'd shove the News of the

Tickles and Rummager who went back to the kennels and died of distemper

World in the bottom of his shoes, 'cause he had holes in his soles and this paper would poke out. He never cared about looks, he just lived for his horses. His nickname in the hunting field was 'legs and wings'. He used to live in the big house on the left, past the bridge in Higham Street. Ben Portway was another farmer who used to hunt he went to Africa as a young man and used to write to me. Mrs Geoff Wear and Miss Pat Freeman also hunted side saddle, in fact Mrs Geoff Wear

always rode in the Point to Point side saddle and Hilda Green followed on foot and was always completely dressed in green.

The Essex and Suffolk Hounds would breed puppies, but they couldn't bring them up, they had to get the farmers to bring them up. Ernie Nunn was the huntsman and he brought over the first one I had who was called Rummager, he was a lovely hound. When they go back they have puppy judging, to see who's walked the best puppy. When Ernie came for Rummager he felt sure I was going to win. I should have won that for the best puppy, but as soon as he got back into the kennels he died. He caught distemper. The next Foxhound I had was General. General was a dear old thing, he was very friendly with a tortoiseshell kitten we'd got. When you went across to the Hollies house, you walked across a path that used to be a driveway at the top of the farm. The cows had been across there and that was like a heap of mud, all of it. General and this little

Ernie Nunn and Mrs Geoff Wear.
photo courtesy of the late Miss Pat Freeman

116

betty kitten were so friendly and there was a little path in the middle where there was not so much mud on and the kitten was walking along there. Then the kitten strayed onto the mud the dog went in the mud picked her up in his mouth and put her back on the path again. I never had anymore Foxhound pups. Only those two. They seemed to catch distemper easily and I did not want any of my Greyhounds getting that.

Ernie Nunn was a great huntsman. He was the only man I know who could call a pack of Foxhounds off a fox when they were in hot pursuit. The hounds loved him, he could do anything with them. Ernie Nunn never married, but he lived with a woman and when they retired they moved down to East Suffolk. Lady Munnings always hunted with the Essex side of the Essex and Suffolk Foxhounds 'cause they split them up into two then - the Essex side and the Suffolk side. Lady Munnings rode side saddle on a grey horse with a groom behind on another identical horse. She used to really go. She was a beautiful horsewoman. Sir

The Essex and Suffolk Point to Point at Bromley in 1924 courtesy of the late Miss Pat Freeman

Alfred used to ride on our side of the Essex and Suffolk Foxhounds because he liked the farmers our way. I remember a Hunt Ball that was held at Hadleigh Town Hall. Dad and I went and Sir Alfred came and asked me for a dance. He couldn't dance at all, he was a terrible dancer, he couldn't walk in step. He kept jumping this way and that, making a mess up of the dance. I kept doing the same anyway. We happened to be near his wife when we were dancing and he said to her: "I've just have a lovely dance with Rosie", he always called me Rosie. She said "have you dear. Well go and have another one will you."

When we were out in the field one day, Sir Alfred said to me: "Go and tell Sir William Burton, the Master, something or other about the fox. So I went on my horse to where he was and said: "Mr Munnings said so and so". He said: "Mr Munnings, Mr Munnings, tell Mr Munnings to pay his hunt subscription fee".

Many years later after I had moved to Newmarket I met old Munnings again on the Heath and he came and looked round our house 'cause he'd been friendly with Frank Wellsman who'd lived there. I gave him some old Dundee marmalade pots which he said were ideal for his brushes and he wanted to buy a big colourman's cabinet of drawers that old Wellsman had his paints in but I would not sell it to him and he often called in after that when he was down Newmarket. When he saw a watercolour that Neil had painted of a horse's head one day he said: "What's that boy doing now, wasting his time on the farm I suppose. He can paint the damned nose and ears better than I can".

Tickles and Colt

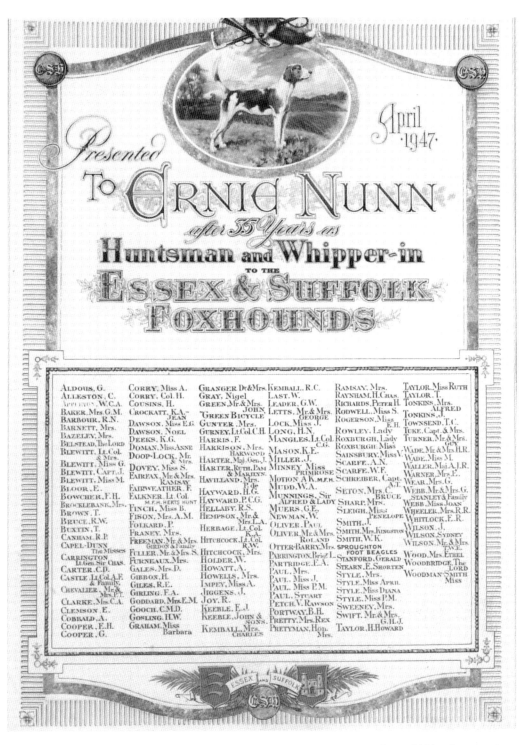

Ernie Nunn's retirement scroll. Dad is the second name down and a lot of our old friends are on here

My tipper-toe-billy-go-lario

I put my hand upon her toe and said what's this me deary
It's me tipper-toe-billy-go-lario, me tipper-toe-billy-go-lario
And every time I tickled me love I'm sure I kissed a fairee

I put my hand upon her foot and said...
It's me broader foot tipper-toe-billy-go-lario...

I put my hand upon her shin and said...
It's me sharper shin, broader foot, tipper-toe-billy-go-lario...

I put my hand upon her knee and said...
It's me knocker knee, sharper shin, broader foot, tipper-toe-billy-go-lario...

I put my hand upon her thigh and said...
It's me thicker thigh, knocker knee, sharper shin, broader foot, tipper-toe-
billy-go-lario...

I put my hand upon her watch and said...
It's me watchagot, thicker thigh, knocker knee, sharper shin, broader foot,
tipper-toe-billy-go-lario...

I put my hand upon her belly and said...
It's me belly gut, watchagot, thicker thigh, knocker knee, sharper shin,
broader foot, tipper-toe-billy-go-lario...

I put my hand upon her breast and said...
It's me milker bags, belly gut, watchagot, thicker thigh, knocker knee,
sharper shin, broader foot, tipper-toe-billy-go-lario...

I put my hand upon her chin and said...
It's me chopper chin, milker bags, belly gut, watchagot, thicker thigh,
knocker knee, sharper shin, broader foot, tipper-toe-billy-go-lario...

I put my hand upon her nose and said...
It's me snotter box, chopper chin, milker bags, belly gut, watchagot, thicker
thigh, knocker knee, sharper shin, broader foot, tipper-toe-billy-go-lario...

I put my hand upon her head and said what's this me deary
It's me cracker box, snotter box, chopper chin, milker bags, belly gut,
watchagot, thicker thigh, knocker knee, sharper shin, broader foot, tipper-
toe-billy-go-lario, me tipper-toe-billy-go-lario
And every time I tickled me love I'm sure I kissed a fairee.

Learned from Sid Hollicks the old horseman of Thorp Morieu who
used to sing it at Polstead Shoulder of Mutton

Chapter 9

I went to my wheat in May and came away not very gay
I went to my wheat in June and came away whistling a tune

Ice in November if that bears a duck, the rest of the winter will
be slush and muck

There's always 20 fine days in November - St Lukes Little
Summer

A hare and a mare go a year (a hare carries its young a month
and a mare eleven months)

Some of Dad's sayings about the weather and life

When I was 16, I finished school and the old man said to me: "What are you going to do?" I said: "I'll stop at home and work on the farm." He said: "Well, you can do that". I stopped at home, then he bought a tractor and I learnt to drive this tractor. Ours was the first International in the area. It was an International Junior and was very, very expensive. When they first came in, Dad said he reckoned that all together, with the equipment and pullies to drive the drum, it had it cost about a thousand pounds. Having got it we had to get someone to teach me to drive it and Miss Muriel Rainsford came to do that. When Tractors came out they reckoned that they were suited to women as they had a seat on.

There were three girls named Rainsford that had a little farm at Assington with their parents. The youngest one, Muriel, went to work for Prettyman. He was an M.P. the other side of Ipswich. He had some farms out there at Trimley, on the way down to Felixstowe and Muriel Rainsford went there to drive their tractor. I don't know why she left. Anyway she came and drove our tractor for a while and taught me. She was an expert at it. Through the sales of International Juniors, they knew all about Miss Rainsford driving a tractor. She was like a land girl. The

tractor came from Brands of Bures. I went to school with two of the Brands. Muriel came and she lived over in the house with us and drove the tractor, she was three or four years older than I was. It would plough two furrows and I drove that tractor for many years.

My International Junior Tractor with my Cockshut Kid Kangaroo Plough

We also had a threshing tackle - a threshing drum, the elevator and a portable steam engine. The steam engine was pulled by horses, so was the drum, and the old man had me taught to drive this steam engine. The engine had a door at the back, a sort of an oval shaped thing with a big wheel at the side, that drove the belt to the drum. It had to have a fire, of course, to heat the water. It had two big wheels and two smaller ones in the front, and things at the side where you used to let the water out and let the water in. I learnt all that before we got the tractor. As we hadn't got a driver for that, we had to borrow somebody from the next door neighbours to come and teach me. The coal used to be shot down the side there. You had to keep putting the coal on the fire and the old boy that taught me to drive, said: "Whatever you do, you must keep your tinder". Your tinder was what the fire was on, "fan and lavel" he said, meaning thin and level. It had a chimney up, you had to get up there and take two bolts out of the chimney and stuff the chimney back down to the main part when you moved it and it needed two horses to pull it. When we bought the International we didn't need that old engine any more. We had a flywheel on the International that you could take off and on and it would drive the drum. I had to be shown how to open the sieves on the drum and let the tail corn through and all that, but I soon learned every job on the farm.

The tractor was bought from Brands of Bures. I think they went broke in the agricultural depression. They came over to collect some money from Dad one time. They knocked on the back door. I said: "I'm sorry but Mr Alleston's in bed". The man said: "He was in bed last time I come".

When Muriel left I used to do the ploughing, for years and years. On a moonlight night I used to go down the field and grease the tractor up, ready for work early in the morning. You used to have to take a knob off and fill it full of grease and put it back on. Never had no nipple guns then. I have been down there with a hurricane lantern - when I was 17 or 18 I suppose - and I would go ploughing by moonlight if the old man wanted to get the field ploughed in a hurry. I'd put a hurricane lantern at either side of the field and plough straight to that. I had a two-furrow trailer plough - it was a Ransome Sims. We also had a Cockshutt Kid Kangaroo, which was horse drawn. That was two furrows and you'd needed three horses to pull it on our land. When we'd finished the ploughing, got the land all up, I could then have a day's hunting on my horse. I always remember Ernie Nunn, when he was huntsman for the Essex and Suffolk. He came over to see the old man and underneath the seat of the tractor was my school bag which had got my food

Muriel Rainsford who had been trained in tractor driving by Brands of Bures. There was an attitude at the time that tractors were for women as they had a seat on them

in and Dad and he were looking in the field where I was working. I was handle harrowing with the tractor. I was drawing these harrows that had handles on the back. When they were horse drawn you could put your weight on the handles at the back to push them in deeper. Ernie asked me about carrying my food. "Oh" I said "I've got my food underneath here, my breakfast, dinner and tea. I won't go home 'till night time" Yes, I didn't go home 'till night time. Ernie was amazed how hard I had to work. I can remember ploughing in Pump Field, as well as can be. I'd plough from the road towards Great Husks hedge, then gather round and back. Even on frosty mornings I could swing the handle on the front round and start her, she was no trouble to start. Muriel Rainsford taught me that you must always keep your thumb on the same side as your fingers when you swing a starting handle. If you don't and it back fires it can break your thumb. If it was cold in the early mornings we'd light a fire under the crank to free the oil up. Muriel later married a Mr Pickering.

I even took the head off and decarbonised her several times. I also decarbonised the old man's six-cylinder Studebaker car once. I did it in the barn when the snow was on the ground, but he called me away to do something else and when I went back to it, it was a job to remember where everything went.

Seated in the air cooled Rover that cost nine pounds

The first car we had was a BSA . Then I bought an air-cooled Rover with Ted Triton because I hadn't enough money. It cost nine pounds, I put up four pounds, we bought it between us. He worked for Ellinger, his father was an auctioneer in Kent. He was an electrician and he lodged with Mrs Rule.

We used to sow with a

Smythe drill then. We'd drill the barley and the artificial manure together, we'd mix it all up together and put it in the drill, or before that we'd drill the wheat and broadcast the artificial by hand. The artificial manure always came from Bunns at Yarmouth.

Then we'd got another little farm at Hadleigh called Fudges Farm, it was one that we hired. The old man planted it all with sugar beet. It was so poor it would not grow the sugar beet no bigger than a carrot, so they left the sugar beet in and let it go to seed. They'd cut the seed off at the root and he wanted to sell the seed. So the seed had to be stacked, so old Harry Tricker and I had to do these things. We had to make stacks over there. You stack one stack one side and one the other and leave sufficient room to put your drum in between. Harry and I went over there to thrash out the seed over at Fudges, so we had to take this great threshing drum with the tractor. It was over 5 miles on those back roads. There was a draw bar on the back of the tractor which drew the drum. Harry rode on the tractor with me. He was looking this way and that to see what wanted to pass and what didn't and he got some logs so when we stopped it we could put a block against the wheel to hold it 'cause this old International tractor didn't have a brake. Harry and I got this blooming great thing round all these corners, down to Fudges, then we got to a place where the road graduated, going up and then you came to a little hill and a sharp turn to the right. The drum weighed tons on the back of this tractor I was driving. Nobody ever thought about there being no brake on the tractor, but as soon as you took the clutch out it would run back. So we were going up this hill and we got up to where you turn right and kept the tractor going, but the tractor couldn't pull all this weight uphill. The tractor wheels went round and they were sinking into the ground; they were iron wheels and they used to have studs that you put on from underneath. Harry was walking behind the drum with these big logs of wood to stop it if anything happened. Of course when the tractor couldn't pull it, the wheels started to spin round. There was only one way to stop the wheels spinning round, that was to put your foot on the clutch. As soon as you put your foot on the clutch, she ran backwards cause there were no brakes to hold her, but Harry was quick with the blocks and we stopped her. He stopped her somehow. Then we filled these holes up in the road and messed about and in the end we had to take the tractor right off and run the tractor forwards and brought it back again on fresh ground, anyway we got there. Do you know, Harry and I we thrashed all that seed out. Then when we started the tractor up you could leave it running like you do with a motor car, leave it ticking over, and Harry used to feed the drum and I used to put the stuff onto the drum for him, the sheaves of sugar beet. I can't remember the journey back with the drum, but we bought the drum back to Red House Farm and Harry and I alone had thrashed all that thirty odd acres of sugar beet seed and carted it back.

Harry was good fun and kept teasing me to try and get a bottle of my home-made wine. He'd had a taste and reckoned that was a drop of good. At Fudgers one day I said: "If you sit on that wasps nest for five minutes you can have a bottle". So he did. He was alright with the wasps trying to get out 'cause his old trousers were so thick but he had a terrible job with the ones trying to get in. Anyway, I said he could have a bottle. His wife was so annoyed with me. She said I could have ruined their marriage.

Harry was with us a long time. He was a bit of a lad and saw the fun in things. On day the old man asked him to get five men for threshing. You could go round and get them how you liked then. A lot sat at home on the dole. Harry came back and said: "I've got 'em guv'nor nineteen men" "Nineteen men Harry what on earth are you thinking about?" He said: "Well I've got Cue Hughes, Dakka Wright, Oscar Marten and Seven Gunn, that's Ten and Niner Gant makes nineteen".

Another time he said: "Old Mrs Green had twenty two children twice". "What never forty four children Harry, she couldn't have done!" "No, no" he said "she had twenty two then she had another one that made twenty three but that died so she had twenty two again.

Chris Smith cycled up from Boxford every day. He had been in the Regular Army before the first world war but had got in tow with a Boxford girl and was constantly going back and getting reported late. On one occasions he told us he was hauled before the CO. "Well what is it this time Smith", said the CO. "It's like this Sir", said Chris, "there I was standing on the platform with my ticket in my hand ready to get on the train when all of a sudden the band struck up God Save the King. Well, me being in uniform, sir, and not wanting to let the Regiment down, I stood to attention and whilst I was immobile, sir, the train left the station". "Smith", said the CO, "you are a credit to the Regiment. Case dismissed - but don't do it again".

Then he deserted altogether and it was the village copper's job to catch him. If anybody saw the copper coming they'd give Chris the lowdown. Like in the pub and that. Chris was sleeping downstairs at this girl's place. The copper came in and stood in the doorway: "I've got you this time Chris", he said, "you can't escape now". "How do you mean you've got me?", said Chris, "when you're over there and I'm over here", and with that he made a dive through the glass of the closed window. Off he made.

Edna and I with a tidy load.
Courtesy of Elizabeth Gardiner, Muriel Rainsford's daughter

Another time the copper was on his bike. He was chasing Chris up Cox Hill. Chris ran into Peartree field where we were cutting with a Sail Reaper. Chris made for the middle of the field to run round behind the Sail Reaper. The copper got off his bike and left it in the gateway. Chris ran right round the corn in the centre of the field and back towards the gate with the copper close behind him. When he came across the copper's bike, "Cheerio", said Chris, as he hopped on it and pedalled down the road leaving the shouting, exhausted copper. Chris had a friend who was a horseman in Cavendish and he used to tell us about when he took his horses home after a storm one night he took them in the horsepond to drink as usual only the electric cable had been blown down into the pond and it electrocuted them all.

Cavendish Cottages. Tommy Doe, a distant cousin, used to farm just behind here

Chapter 10

Oh the old Iron Cross, the old iron cross its a laugh I do declare
Over there in Germany they are giving them away
You can get a couple if you shout hooray
The Kaiser shouted meat, meat, meat
I gave him some of course
T'was only a nibble of me old ham bone
But he gave me the old iron cross

I think I got this from Harry Tricker

About the same time as I left school, I decided I wanted to learn ballroom dancing. I had always been keen on dancing, having learned at Madame Beard's at Hadleigh, but ballroom dancing was all the go then and I wanted a go. So Dad took me down to a dancing class that was held at the Rose and Crown at Sudbury. Sometimes he would take me or if he didn't, I'd bike and Maud Haggis would bike with me 'cause she came from Edwardstone and she was learning as well, but that was a long way - about six miles. The Rose and Crown was burnt down in the '30s, but that was a lovely old Hotel where Charles Dickens had stayed, and that had a big open hall inside with a gallery all the way round. Anyway, I went down there and learned ballroom and Old Time Dancing.

But, of course, the next thing was that Dad wanted to learn 'cos there was dances everywhere round then. So he decided to buy a gramophone and, as the Hollies Farmhouse was not lived in, we went over there and lit a fire and put the gramophone on and I had to teach him. I taught him the waltz and things like that, and did the Valeta and Maud Haggis would come up and Edna would come over, and perhaps one or two others. In fact, afterwards, at one of these dances Dad won a waltzing competition. There were village dances that time of day all round. We used to go to Groton, Polstead and Boxford Village Halls. Then there'd be other dances upstairs at the room at The Fleece in Boxford, or they'd hold balls at the Victoria Hall at

Sudbury, or at Hadleigh Town Hall there'd be a Hunt Ball, or a Farmers' Ball. If Dad wanted to go he'd try and get some tickets. Mum didn't go so I was allowed to go with him instead.

I remember a lot of these dances were for charity; mostly raising money for the soldiers that had been Prisoners of War or injured in the war. At one at Boxford Fleece, that was upstairs, I heard Claude Morgan was going to be there. He was good looking and he'd been away and been one of a crew of an Airship. They used to live in Sudbury and they had moved to Boxford. His mother was a widow and she had two boys, Eddy and Claude. Eddy had been killed in the war. Claude was two years younger and was determined to avenge the death of his brother, so he joined up. He was 18 but I was only 16. He'd been somewhere the other side of Bedford. Cardington I think it was called, on the R101. After the war he had been discharged. When he came out of the war he had a little money and he bought a Ford Pickup, and used to do a bit of carting and that like for people. But I was 16 I remember and had got my hair down, and I was afraid he wouldn't notice me, so I put it up in 'earphones' like in the photograph, and he did dance with me. I met him one or two times after that, and he used to walk home with me from Boxford up to Red House Farm but not if Dad knew it! Anyway, he was always at the dances and we got on well.

I had my hair done in headphones in case Claude Morgan was there

His mother lived in Boxford. There used to be a girl come over from Sudbury every weekend and stay there. She was a funny looking girl I reckoned. When I got to know him more I asked him why she'd come over. He used to say: "That's my Mother. She asks her over to come and spend the weekends with us, because she's only got her father, her mother has died". If she was staying there at the weekend and there was a dance on the Saturday night, he would still come to the dance, but he never brought her. My father used to criticise him all he could and say nasty things about him. One night I saw him and we had to dodge the old man. One morning, I was going to meet him and he was going to walk home with me Thursday night. When I went to Boxford in the morning to get something, somebody said: 'Claude's got married'. He was married that morning down at the Register office at Hadleigh. He married the girl that kept going up to his mother's, she was pregnant. They called the baby Molly Morgan, then he had to provide for the lot of them. He got a house in Boxford, he took me up to his mother's house to see the baby and his wife was quite friendly.

There was a dance I went to with Dad at The Bull at Long Melford, where they had a dance hall upstairs. I danced with Claude there and his friend Ted Eady, who was in the auctioneers office at Sudbury. They used to get together those two and do a turn at the concerts around. Ted Eady's favourite song was 'The end of me old cigar'. Anyway, at that dance, Dad kept popping downstairs for a drink 'cos there wasn't any in the dance hall. He was getting quite tight, and I was scared to go home with him.

I went to a dance at Kersey once when they had a concert. They asked me down there and Jack Stiff made a rare fuss of me. I did the Highland Fling. Jack was about my age. Jack Stiff was the son of Robert Stiff. Robert Stiff died at an early age and there was Mrs Stiff left. She had three sons, Cecil, Antham and Jack. Jack was the youngest one. Cecil married a girl I used to go to school with. Antham had several sons. Jack and Antham ran the General Stores in Kersey and he used to cure hams, but they weren't as good as mother's. They used to cure them in black treacle and Jack had a van and it had everything written on it. You could buy paraffin from the back, saucepans on the front, everything and it used to call on you.

The Gages were also at the dances. They were Leonard Gage's children, they lived at Common Farm, Semer. Blanche the eldest one, when she left school went on to be a nurse in Leicester and there she stayed until she died. George the next one, was a little older than me, he eventually went to a family out in Ireland.

Nora was the next one, she married a farming dealer locally. Frank went to the war. Harry went to work for the machinery people who did the Claas combines. Frank did not forgive his father for selling the farm whilst he was away in the last war. His mother lived in that last cottage in Kersey street that Harry Aggis the Pork Butcher had and that is always being photographed. He treated her badly. He was as mean as buggery. After Nora came home she got friendly with Jack Stiff.

Whenever I wanted to go out the old man always wanted to come to these dances. He was always looking and finding out who I was dancing with - he was a damn nuisance. One night, when I went with Edna and a girl who was mother's help at the time, he followed on and came to a dance in Polstead and because we did not take any notice or dance with him he went off home. When we got back he had locked the door, and we had to sleep in a haystack and that was old stovver hay which was coarse and uncomfortable.

I met Freddy Theobald dancing; he asked me for a dance somewhere and I suppose I danced well and he kept on dancing with me. One night when I went down to the Victoria Hall, Sudbury, with Dad and Edna, there was a big competition on. It was the Eastern Counties' cup and Freddy Theobald was supposed to be entering with his girlfriend. He said: "I won't be able to dance with you, Ru, for the cup. I have got to dance with my late girlfriend", a girl he was engaged to and I used to go to school with her. He said: "She's coming down here especially to dance with me for the cup". Anyway, my Father and my sister, Edna, went up on the balcony. I was dancing with Freddy in the dance before the cup and he kept saying: "She hasn't arrived yet" this girlfriend of his. They started dancing, all the couples with their numbers pinned on their backs and still this girl hadn't arrived. We were sitting and waiting so Freddy said: "Ru, you'll have to dance now", I said: "No I'm not, you wait for that girlfriend and see if she comes". Well, they got on the floor and they were dancing and still she hadn't come so he jumped up and pinned a number on the back of my dress and said: "Come on, let's have a go". There were ten judges and it was for a waltz, a quick step and a slow fox- trot. They were dancing away and the dancing was half over by the time we got in the floor. A Haverhill couple won the waltz with 75%. So we are on the floor for the next one which is the fox-trot and we won the fox-trot with 100%, then the next dance after that was the slow fox-trot and we won that with 100%, so we won two out of the three. That was the Eastern Counties Cup and the silk factory gave us individual prizes and I had an evening handbag and we got the Challenge Cup and Freddy daren't take it home. His father kept a little pub not far from Sudbury grammar school. He was to keep it for six months and I was to keep it for six months, but he daren't take it home in case his girlfriend came down and seen he'd won the cup. He said she'd smash it. So I had it all the time and I had his and my name put on.

He came over the farm to see me after that, he kept pestering. I knew what he was after, but I said: "Oh no", and I never saw him any more after that. Freddy gave Tickles a fox terrier called Nip and it was not long after that he was killed. He picked up with another girl in Sudbury somewhere, he got married and I think they had two children. He was driving some horses from one paddock to another one and they had to cross the road. This bus came along as he was shooing horses out of the road and he slipped on the pavement and fell in front of the bus which ran over him and killed him.

The Eastern Counties Dance cup that I won with Freddy Theobald

Mrs Jordan used to come to the dancing classes during World War 1. The Jordan's were coal merchants in Sudbury. There was an aeroplane come down in that big pit on the Newton Green road out of Sudbury where there are some cottages on the side. Mrs Jordan came down. She lived on the bank on the other side of the road; when she came down she picked the pilot's head up in the road and put it in her apron. She was no more good after that, that affected her.

My dear old Nabs lead by Nip crossing from the Hollies Farm

Chapter 11

Now me one man, me two men they all mow together
Me three men, me four men they carry me grass away
With my four, my three, my two, my one they all work well
They mow me hay, they carry it away they are all jolly fine
fellows

As sung in Boxford White Hart by George Smith publican and Thatcher. He was Tonardo's father. That goes on until it reaches 100 but he'd stop after about twenty.

I met George Smith again, after many years, at one of the dances in Boxford. I had known him since I danced at the end of the war celebrations and he was in the Scouts, and we had both been Confirmed together at Edwardstone.

His father kept the White Hart and he used to go out thatching as well, thatching all day. He had a pony cart that used to stand and wait. First of all they lived at White Street Green, just after the 1914-1918 war. I hadn't got a particular boyfriend and I used

George 'Tonardo' Smith the Wall of Death Rider

to go down to the dances with Edna or anyone else. They used to have a dance at Boxford Village Hall about once a month. One evening I was down there and he danced with me. He had a AJS motorbike then. I arranged to meet him on the top of Sand Hill out of Boxford going towards Hadleigh. We walked down Shakers Hall Lane. I left my bike by the side of the road, and we walked all down the back way by the stream, down towards the pub down Stone Street, The Compasses, and then we walked back. He was ever such good company and I was very fond of him. My Father didn't approve of him. He was just a lad from the village so to make sure that he didn't know where I was. I used to go off in the other direction, instead of coming down to Boxford, which was a short cut, and up Sand Hill to meet him. Every fellow I had he was always against every time I went out anywhere. I've known the time when someone would pick me up in a taxi and take me to a dance at Sudbury and Dad would come too!! He hadn't been asked, but he'd be all ready when the man came.

I used to go up to where Mary Towns lived at the four cross road at Kersey Tye, and turn right there, down the back, right round Kersey Tye, past The Brewers Arms and turn to the right and come that way round. I met him there lots of times. During that time, Dad got onto me and I used to run away when I was going out with George. I went over and stayed at Easthorpe Hall and George came over to see me there. Nellie Doe lived there, I could always go there. Nellie Doe was Mother's cousin. Nellie Doe's mother and my Mother's mother were sisters. George came to see me on his motor bike, I really looked forward to that. Easthorpe Hall was near Marks Tey, Colchester way.

A letter from George

When it all finished was when we went to a dance in Boxford in the Village hall and at the end of the dance, Edna was there and my Old Man came. He said: "You're coming home with me Ru". "I'm not", I said: "I'm going home with George". "He's not going to bring you home", he started to create and make a fuss. It didn't matter where he was, if he was riled at me he would swear at me in front of anybody. I told George that I would have to go home with my Father otherwise he would lock me out. He said: "Don't take any notice of him Ru, I'll take you home". He kept vowing he would take me home and I had Dad saying he was going to take me. I made the biggest mistake of my life that night, I went home with my Father. If I'd had gone home with George, the old man would have chucked me out, then that would have been the end. I'd have been free and away. However I never saw George any more after that except when we were both married. That annoys me all the new people now calling him Tonaydo when his name is Tonardo.

Nellie Doe of Easthorpe Hall. She had a sister Leggie and Brothers George, Albert and Tom. Tom was father of Rowley, Jack, Eleanor and Tommy Doe who Farmed at Cavendish

All the time I went out with him we kept scheming to make money, so we could get away. He was going to get on the Wall of Death at Whitby, Yorkshire. Then his time came, he went to work for some people who ran a Wall of Death. He went there as a mechanic. He got on the Wall and he was brilliant. The man who he worked for sent him abroad to Sweden and Holland and other countries to ride on the Wall. When he got back here he went to Southend and he made a lot of money. He used to go back up to London at Christmas time - they had a big do at the White City where he rode on the Wall of Death in Bertram Mills Circus. There he met his wife. They bought a lion cub which used to sit on the

Tonardo and Lion

handlebars while he went round the Wall. He also had his own house built at Southend. It was all oak inside. While he was still at Southend he built a yacht himself because he wanted to sail round the world. People were jealous of him and he only just finished it when

someone set fire to it. One night when he came to Boxford, to the White Hart and the lion was in one of the boxes and he heard it making a funny noise. He went over to it and it was hung up and had broken a leg in its box, so he had to shoot it. They buried it outside the Hart in front of the window.

Dad locked me out once when I was with him. George said I was a fool to stop at home and that I needed a trade and it was because of him that I went hairdressing. Claude Morgan used to say that as well. When I finished with George I was so upset that I thought I would do something different. I would take up hairdressing. It was all over between us, he had been away doing the wall. I was still at the farm when he came back and I was introduced to George's wife, Doris. She was very, very well dressed. Now George was famous Dad would listen to him, particularly as he realised he was making a lot of money. George was building this caravan. He was friendly with the Alstons. The Alstons had a big shop in Sudbury. Old Mr Alston was Mayor of Sudbury. He had two sons, Roy and Les, he also had another brother who died. When his brother died he left everything to his brother's eldest son, Les, so Les had a bigger share in the business than his father - that's why Les was boss. Roy married my best friend, Sibyl Dansie. Mrs Dansie was a school teacher at Boxford and Mr Dansie was an undertaker in Boxford. He was friendly with Tonardo. Les Alston spread out, he went to Ipswich and bought a place. Eventually his factory covered a big piece of land that was called the Oboe - it was an acre.

After his father died I remember dancing with Roy. When I was at the cottage in Boxford, I went to Alston's in Sudbury to buy some lino. I paid for it, but I had no one to lay it, so Roy came over and laid it for me.

When the war was on, Tonardo went into the fire service; he became a fireman and his wife was also something to do with it. She got friendly with the Governor and she ran away with him.

George used to play the piano in the pub - he was gifted. He never had a music lesson. He wrote poetry for me and sent it me.

George used to drive a taxi at Felixstowe in the summer. He always went down there and he stayed at Bath House. George liked a joke. They pulled him for speeding in Felixstowe so he went down the Fort and paid his fine in pennies. He paid four pound's worth in pennies and a pound's worth in farthings. He picked up one farthing and took it back and put in back in his pocket. He told the Clerk of the Court that he would have to count it all again. He rode there on a penny farthing bicycle with an 'L' plate up.

When he got on the Wall, George saved his money and he bought two thousand pound's worth of Marks and Spencers shares and he continued to save. They said he was mean, but he wasn't mean, he just took care of it, care of his money. When he got money, other people were jealous of him. My rotten old father upset me after all he'd said about him. When George asked him to look at his caravan, he went down there and sat with him with a glass of port wine. His wife was there and I was there too - it was embarrassing for me.

Liz, George's mother, was at home in the Hart of course. She had another son, John, who was very near George's age, then she went a long time and had two more, Stan and Basil. She was very kind to anybody who really needed it. On a Saturday night she used to make a huge beef steak pudding. In the hard times when all the old boys used to go in there and buy a pint off her on a Saturday night, she used to give them all some beef steak pudding free of charge. They were a very popular couple and they kept the pub for thirty years. Sometimes in there they would do a step dance called 'Jack's the Lad'. Reg Fletcher played his Akordeen for it. It's a squeezebox with buttons either side, not a concertina and not an accordion which has piano keys. The old boys all called it an Akordeen and it had four stops on top that you had to pull up to let the sound out. I did not go in there too much. In that time of day it was mostly men and on a Saturday night I was not allowed out, but I'd go down there sometimes when I lived in Boxford. They would sing in there on a Saturday night. Old George's party piece was 'me one man, me two man, they all work together' and Roly Fletcher's was 'Bungay Roger'.

When I fell out with Dad once, Mrs Charles Kembell was a dear and took me in straightaway. She said: "I've got a little bedroom at the back you can have." She lived at Cox Farm with her husband and I stayed there for two weeks. Charles Bumper Kemball was her husband. He was the Judge at Sudbury and District and Colchester and District Coursing Clubs. He used to get so tight when he was MC at the whist drives. One night when he went to announce the trumps he said "Hearts are diamonds," meaning to say "trumps." When anyone asked what the trumps were that always seemed to come out, even years later. They had four children, the eldest was Richard, then there was Betty, who was a school teacher. She married Edward Wendon who was a bank manager in Soham. Then Jack and several years passed then there was Mary. Mary married Titch Wheeler from Sudbury, they had sawmills and Mary, much later, was Godmother to Neil, my son, who's getting these stories together.

Dick Kemball age 21 and Ben Hogger the Boxford Coffin maker

I went to school with Richard at Miss Byers school in Hadleigh. He sometimes used to ride a bike but sometimes rode a horse. As soon as he was old enough he went to Sudbury Grammar school. Then he went to an agricultural institution at Chadacre. When he left there he went straight to Paul Oliver's, the auctioneers, to manage his farms. Paul Oliver had been a pupil auctioneer with Charles Boardman in Haverhill and Charles Boardman had started him off auctioneering in Sudbury where they had formed the very successful partnership Boardman & Oliver. Ted Eady, of that firm, who I'd met at dances years before with Claude Morgan, always used to do Dad's work if he wanted any valuing done or anything like that, but mostly we sold our cows at Spurling & Hempson or Bonds in Ipswich. There were always good prices at Stowmarket pig auctions where Woodwards and RC Knights had big sales. Dick Kemball managed Oliver's farms at Waldingfield and he also used to deal in horses as well and provide horses for the hunt. He was great fun, Dick, always pulling your leg. I don't think that Jack was there when I stayed and one of the last times I saw Jack then was on Cox Hill and he said to me: "I don't know Ruby what I shall do if I don't get a job soon, I shall go to Australia". About that time a lot of boys were going to Australia. There was a whole mob of them from Boxford, Toby Munson was one, two boy Trickers, Alby and Alfy, John Goody and another boy from Stone Street. When they landed out there, they were supposed to go out to work on farms, but there didn't seem much for them to do and jobs were hard to find, and the boy Goody went to work for a baker and confectioner. He had been an apprentice in that trade to a man named Griggs in Boxford so he was alright. Toby Munson came back for a holiday and one of the Trickers worked on an apple farm, but just for a holiday. Jack didn't go, he then managed a farm for Sainsbury's at Layham, but some time after that he took a lot of light land down at Butley in East Suffolk, blowing sand it was. No one else could make a go of it but Jack did. Anyway they were all good sorts and I knew them real well and they had no hesitation in taking me in. Charles Kemball's father was Bumper Kemble the judge at the Coursing Clubs. Dick Kemble was very kind to me. When I got into trouble with the old man he allowed me to turn my horse out on one of their paddocks. Dick was very friendly with Joshua Hulme - they called him Joe Hum - and another chap called Jimmy Lindley. After Jimmy married he moved into Willow Farm, Assington where my Mother's aunt and uncle had lived but I never saw him after that, and Jimmy didn't live to be a very old man. I knew them well 'cause they used to play football and when they said they would be playing at Boxford I would go down on my horse and watch them. Claude Morgan, Bert Cook, Sid Rainham and one of the Gunns all played in the Boxford team. Another old character that we used to meet in the markets, or driving her horse and cart on the road, was Jemima Godfrey and although she died in the 1920s there was a post with her name on it on the main road right up until the fifties.

Jemima Godfrey who farmed Godfrey's Farm, Assington. photo courtesey of Godfrey Tabiner

Old Ben Hogger was a carpenter who lived in Swan Street and he used to make the coffins for old Mr Kemble. Where they used to put the bodies in the coffins was on the corner of Butchers Lane. He used to sell oil as well, I used to go there and buy oil for my father to make drinks for horses - linseed oil. It used to come off his loft where he kept the coffins. Linseed oil would stop the belly ache. You could give cows linseed oil as well. They used to put some ginger in or something. When they give a horse a drink they have a bottle with a long strong neck. I used to stand in the manger, put a rope over the beam, and put it round the horse's head and pull the horse's head up. When I got the horse's head up straight, I'd get a man to hold the horse over towards me, then I'd put the long-necked bottle, or a drenching horn, down the side of the mouth and give the horse a drink. If that didn't cure it you'd send for the vet. They'd keep laying down if they had belly ache. If it got a twisted gut they would have to put it down - there was no cure. I had to have a thoroughbred mare put down with that in my later life. When they put an old horse or a too docile horse in a sale they would put a piece of ginger up its backside. The horse would come in the sale ring all sprightly then. That's where the expression 'gingered up' comes from.

Anyway I went up to the Kembles for a few days and after things subsided and Dad was alright, I crept back home again and that's how it went on. Usually things were better after a few days.

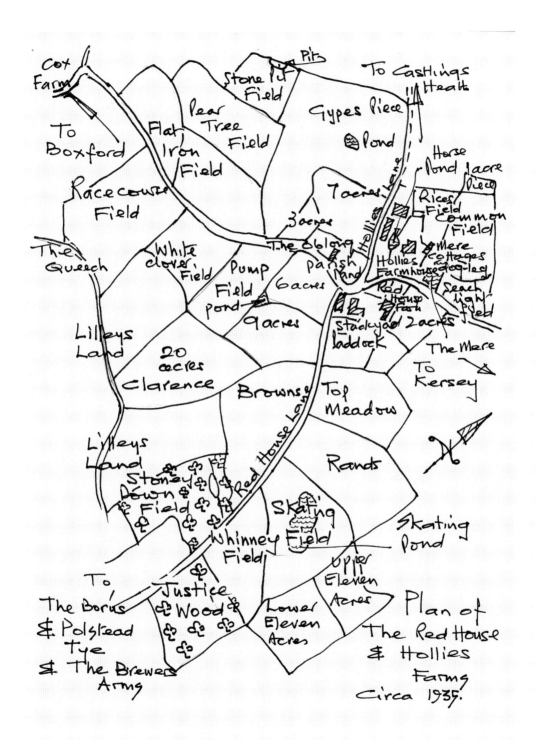

Cot Farm

To Boxford

Stone Pit
Pit
Stone Pit Field

Pear Tree Field

Flat Iron Field

Gypes Piece
Pond

To Castlings Heath

Horse Pond
1 acre Piece

7 acres

3 acres

The Oblong

Rices Field
Common Field

Mere Cottages

Racecourse Field

The Queech

White Clover Field

Pump Field Pond

6 acres

Parish Land

Hollies Farmhouse
Dog-leg

Red House Frank

Seach
Lion Field

9 acres

Stackyard
Paddock

2 acres

The Mere

Lilleys Land

20 acres

Clarence

Brownse

Top Meadow

To Kersey

Lilleys Land

Stoney Down Field

Red House Lane

Rands

Skating

Skating Pond

Whinney Field

Upper Eleven Acres

To The Borus
& Polstead Tye
& The Brewers Arms

Justice Wood

Lower Eleven Acres

Plan of
The Red House
& Hollies
Farms
Circa 1935.

Gallant Bendor

We took him down to the Epsom Course
Where the bookies said 'he's a fine horse'
But his jockey, he is injured, so it's a ten to one we'll lay
He'll never beat the champion, and win the prize this day

He's a chestnut horse grand and neat
A chestnut horse four pretty little feet
So success to Gallant Bendor
And shout me lads hurray
For he beat the cracks at Epsom
And he bore the prize away

Now Archers arm had been crushed, savaged by a wicked hoss,
Of all the famous jockeys, bold Archer is the king,
But he'll never ride a finish with his arm tied in a sling

When they came up the hill, Freddy Archer he sat still
When they reached Tattenham Cornerm he to the Bendor did say
"Pick up your feet my beauty, and we'll win the prize this day"

So he lay Bendor upon the rail and up that hill he never did fail
And though Robert the Devil had left them far behind
They overhauled that champion to winning the last stride

Now though they're gone and lie beneath some see them ride across the heath
Riding again to victory like the year of '83
When they won that Epsom Derby in a feat of gallantry

Learned by Dad from an old boy in The Anchor at Nayland before
the 14-18 war. I've never heard it anywhere else.

Chapter 12

In the early 20s things kept getting worse and worse. Times were bad. The plaster was falling off Hollies Farm and when a big bit fell off the front, it exposed the beams and Dad was worried about this so he asked Bloss Kingsbury in Boxford to give him a price to do the Hollies house up. He said it would cost £2,000. Dad could not afford anything hardly at all so he advertised it for sale. Not far across the meadow were two cottages, they were called The Mere Cottages. One of them you had to step over a beam to get into the bedroom, that's how old they were. They both had lovely gardens, big gardens. The old man couldn't sell the Hollies house, he didn't think it was very saleable, then one of the cows walked into the back of one of the cottages and knocked the plaster off down there. So he said: "I'll sell that if I could". I said: "How much do you want for it?" He said: "Fifty pounds". I said: "I'll have it". I said, "You owe me £25 that you borrowed the other day, I'll give you the other £25". He still wanted to sell the Hollies house and someone came along from the other side of Ballingdon and offered him £350 for the house and the pair of Mere Cottages, also the front meadow, the four-acre back meadow and the orchard. So the old man sold it to him. He said to me: "Ru you can't have the cottage after all because the man that bought the house wouldn't buy it without the cottages". To my father's disgust this man who bought the house knocked the rest of the plaster off the house and did a

The Hollies Farm House, now called Wicker Street House

little to the roof, then he offered if for sale again - the front off an all. A man called Letts bought it - he was a landscape gardener and set the garden out lovely. He was there a few years and he had a sale there and in that sale the old man bought the pedal- roller (photo on back cover). It was wonderful to sit on a roller and pedal it and I suppose Letts bought it because he wanted to be up on all the latest things. No one wanted it at his sale though because it was such hard work, so Dad gave next to nothing for it and it was then put against the back wall of the house where it stayed for years. It had been patented by a man A.S.F. Robinson of Barsham, near Beccles and was a wonderful idea because it had two gears and when you turned, it had a mechanism that threw one half of the back roller out of gear for easy turning. I've never seen another like it and nor has anyone else, I have been led to believe. It is extraordinary though how it never went for scrap. It is marvellous how they didn't let it go to Lightning Lock, the Scrapman. He used to call round every week. In the Second World War when I lugged the tail of the doodlebug that landed in Garnet Lilleys field back up to the farmyard, that stood there about a month then Dad let Lightning Lock have it for scrap. Old Lightning used to stand on the hill outside The Swan at Melford on a Saturday night and would take anyone on bare fist for a pound.

He got into the Suffolk Regiment in the war and fought for the Regiment - he had great long arms and a big reach. After the war Weller-Pooley the Commander Officer, said to Bob Chapman his foreman 'Find old Lightning some work if you can' because Chapman didn't want him up there. So Chapman said "Lightning meet me at the Estate Office and I'll find you some 'tarmacadaming.'" It's up at such and such a farm says Chapman. So way Lightning goes in his halfbuck lorry putting his right-hand out of the right window to turn right and his left hand out of the left window to turn left. 'There it is Lightning' says Chapman 'put two coats on that roof and come and tell me when you're done'. Well in about half an hour Lightning was up there for his money. 'You can't have finished' says Chapman 'I'll come and see'.

On seeing the roof "you haven't put two coats on there", says Chapman. "Yes I have" says Lightening "I put the two coats on together at the same time".

Wheat got more and more difficult to sell, no one seemed to want it and the old man's temper got worse with it. They used to reckon in farming the price of a sack of corn paid a man's weekly wage. Well corn was going off the farm then for as little as 10 shillings a sack and the men - not that anyone coveted what they were getting - were paid 25 to 30 shillings a week. That's an 18-stone sack of wheat, because barley measures 16 stone a sack and oats 12-stone. Corn was all stored in sacks once it was thrashed. Our old sacks the men had to mend with sack needles, then it all had to be carried out of the barn and I've carried it as well, but the men would not let me carry an 18-stone sack of wheat. 12-stone of oats or a 16-stone sack of barley was enough. I had to do every job there was on the farm. After the corn was cut in the field, they all had to be shocked up and that was usually done first thing in the morning. We would go out and pick up the sheaves of corn and they would be full of Scotsmen - those big old sow thistles so you got all sorts of things in your hand that would fester. If there had been a dag you'd get wet

Boxing match at the Suffolk Yeomanry Camp

through so you had to have an old sack hanging in front tied with a piece of binder string around you. They used to cut the straw long that time of day. If you went round behind a binder there would be all sort of little creatures there like big old harvest spiders or nests of field mice, rannies and frogs and toads in the corn, voles or little pheasant chicks and I can even remember the men talking about a Corncrakes being in the corn when I was very young 'cause they were very rare then. Little birds used to run about in the corn but none of those creatures will go in there now. There would be milky doe rabbits that would make a shallow burrow, hardly under the ground then have their young ones in there and if you caught them you couldn't sell them, no one would want to buy a milky doe.

People used to come round gleaning, they'd rake up the straw. To stop people going in those fields we'd have to leave a 'policeman'. That's a couple of sheaves of corn bound together in the middle, and that would tell them they couldn't go in there yet 'cause they always used to rake up the corn after that had been cleared, and sometimes that would take almost 'til Christmas to get it done. The men used to get paid extra for harvest. They didn't get any overtime rate then but they'd work extra hours. We'd never ever worked on a Sunday and no one else ever did. Religious or not they all respected the Sabbath.

Harry Tricker could do anything, he used to thatch all the stacks. I've thatched as well. Harry used to thatch with wheat straw, you'd damp the straw down then you'd pull it. I've pulled straw all day and put it into yolks for Harry. Harry would put it in a piece of wood with a long rope on and they'd put these yolks in and tie it up. I'd cart it up the ladders onto the stack. They'd make these ropes - wisps of straw with a thing with a handle that they called a 'spud'. They used hazel brauchers. They would cut hazel sticks out the hedge and split them up so they could twist them and they'd bend 'cause hazel wouldn't snap. After Harry Tricker finished we had Chris Smith do the thatching. Most of the Smiths round Boxford were thatchers. On the last load of sheaves that came out of the harvest field, we used to ride home on top of a load with a big green bough that the men called 'the harvest bough'. We always brought the green bough home on the last load. As soon as ever harvest was over they'd start ploughing if they could. They always used to reckon on this heavy land you should get it all ploughed up before Christmas so the frost could get to it. They farmed with nature that time of day not agin it. You'd lay as much of your land open to the surface so the frost could get to it and break it down to tilth and they'd plant anything they could in the Autumn, or, if they'd plant spring barley they would often 'under sow it'. That meant that they'd plant clover later so the clover would grow but it would not be high enough to cut when the barley was harvested 'cause the straw was a lot longer that time of day. When the land in the spring is just drying out they'd call that 'hazening'. They'd said that in the old days the old boys would take their trousers down and test the temperature of the land with their buttocks to see if it was ready to drill. Oats would stand in the field on the shock so they heard the church bells for three Sundays before they were carted.

My mother - Emily or Cack, as we called her, in the front garden

I've ploughed acres and acres with horses. 'Cup a wee and wardee' you'd say if you want at the end of a furrow for them to turn right or left. When old Billy Simpson was horseman, he was a real old timer and if there was a new foal born on the farm he used to get the afterbirth and spread it over a hedge. It was always a blackthorn hedge. These old horsemen reckoned that as the young leaves grew through, so the foal would grow. I think that was the idea about that, but all the old horsemen did it.

We had a three quarter bred shire horse that I used to plough with and one day when the meet was local I said to Dad: "I'm going Hunting tomorrow; I'm taking the day off". "You can't go Hunting" he said "you've nothing to ride". "Well" I said, "I'm going on the three quarter shire I was ploughing with today" and I went.

If the hounds came past, the horses used to get ever so excited; they would just as likely try and get out. Smart got out when the hounds went past one day and she got stuck in a ditch and strained herself and could not stand. So we went back and lifted a big door off the barn and took that down and got it under her. We then dragged her back into the barn on this door. We got her in the barn and got slings and a canvas underneath her and slung her up to the beams on tackle, so it took all the weight off her legs and she got better and got over it.

In the front garden of the Red House there were all sorts of nut trees there, Filberts, Cobs and Hazels - they'd be ready about harvest time and I think they had been there since the house was built in Georgian times. We all used to get in there with mother and get as many as we could, we would put them in stone jars or sometimes in a biscuit tin, then we would bury then in a hole in the ground and they'd keep like that 'til Christmas. New potatoes will keep like that too.

Tickles, when he was a young boy, was always climbing a tree after something or other. He had a pigeon when he as a boy and that was called Poor Boy and it used to speak like that and say 'poor boy'. This pigeon would suddenly fly down and sit on your shoulder. When they had fireworks one year it got frightened and never came down anymore. Once when he was up a nut stub someone said a squirrel was coming, he was so frightened he fell out.

Boxford Fair was about harvest time, Mrs Creighton used to run it, she was the old lady of the fair and that was held about the second weekend in September. There would be all sorts of things there, a steam roundabout, there would be gallopers, the jollity farm and the cakewalk. Later Mrs Creighton married a Bugg and they came from Stoke. They used to do all the fairs round about and in winter time they used to winter their equipment in the White Hart yard. There were two Creighton boys and they would work locally in the winter going sugar beeting and that like and one of them went to work for Rule's, driving Rules' buses. When they had a fair at Stoke, all the fair people had to go into the church before they were allowed to operate the fair. There used to be a big horse fair many years ago in Stoke and the fair was held right the way through the street. The old men reckoned that Stoke Fair was the right time for planting your runner bean seed. That was held on the second weekend in May - usually about Rook Shooting day which is 12th May and there was an old custom that the fairground men had to go into the church to a special service before the Fair could be opened.

When Claude was in Stoke one day, he hurt his arm badly and the old man would not take him to hospital. He went into the pub there, The Angel, that was kept by Tonardo Smith's brother. "Well boy", he says, "You ought to go to hospital and have it X-rayed". Claude replied he had no one to take him. So the landlord said: "I'll take you". So he took him up to hospital and waited for him while he had it x-rayed and set and bought him home again. Claude said: "How much am I in your debt?" Smith said: "That's all right boy, you don't owe me nothing".

Alb Baker used to work on the farm, his sister was Liz Smith who kept The White Hart. He was Tonardo's uncle and he used to have a motor bike and he used to get up to poaching. In fact, he had been in Norwich jail with his friend Doubleup Griggs who also worked on the farm at various times. They got caught several times. Doubleup, when he was a young man, used to have a cottage on the edge of Bulls Cross Wood and he lived there and he had a sister. He used to go in the wood and poach pheasants at night time. No-one caught him there but one night he went out Aga Fenn way and they reckoned the gamekeepers

Tickles first starting to ride

got wind that they were going there and, as they jumped over a gate into the wood, so a number of them set upon them and beat them up. Doubleup was a bit of a fighter too and so was Al, but they did them over. Old Doubleup wasn't scared of anyone. One night he went to the village dance hall where he was known to be a bit of a troublemaker and Bloss Kingsbury, who was a local builder, was on the door. He looked over the top of his glasses and said: "You can't come in here Griggs. We are not having the likes of you in here". "Well" said Doubleup: "I've been in woods and all sorts of places in the middle of the night, but I've never been frightened by a b..... owl yet, so here's my money I'm coming in".

Old Doubleup was always smoking Churchman Counter roll ups. He'd say 'Don't you make a niase' meaning 'don't you make a noise' - don't tell anyone about it and Tickles was always taking

Brother Claude, Polly Rice's boy, Blossom, Tickles and Reg Fletcher

him off. He'd also say 'no bumming' if something was meant to be the truth. 'No bumming boy no bumming'.

Reg Fletcher's mother used to keep The Brewers Arms which was down the bottom of the lane on the Polstead side past the Bo'rus where Garnet Lilly farmed. They had to come out of there in the hard times and Dad let them have one of the Hollies cottages. Reg used to help on the farm. If he hadn't got any work he would always sit outside and play his squeeze box. It was lovely to sit on the gate by The Mere and hear the music coming over the field. He used to sing as well, one of his songs I remember was The Wild Rover.

Land got cheaper and you couldn't sell anything. Nobody had got any money and nobody wanted to buy anything. You could rent almost any land you liked rent free for three years. They said that you could walk on land from Clacton to Cambridge that nobody would take. It just stood derelict and became scrub. We put more land down to grass and had cows and sold the milk. In those days it was about one and two pence halfpenny for a gallon. We had to pay the carriage on the milk. We would take the milk to the station on the square cart, (the one that Dad had when he just started as a hay dealer), pulled by a grey pony. You had to leave about quarter past seven to get the eight o'clock train from Hadleigh. If anybody was away I would drive it down.

Anyway, as the wheat price was so bad and you could still sell the milk, Dad put more land down to grass and hired some grazing the other side of Sudbury at Gestingthorpe. We then had to get these horses and some cows over to Gestingthorpe to be turned out. It was winter time and this man over there was taking them in at so much a head and we had 30 dry cows. That was a lovely morning when they went out, not a sign of snow or anything. The man hadn't been gone very long, when it suddenly started to snow, it was fine snow and it all laid and kept on comin' down. When it got to six o'clock at night, somebody came up the farm and said that the cows that were to end up at Gestingthorpe were all the way along the road, here, there and everywhere. They had slipped over, they couldn't stand on those slippery roads. One lay here, and one lay there. One old cow tried to get up - she tried and tried then couldn't try any more. The old man said I had better take his big old Studebaker to see what I could do. So off I went to herd these cows, Dad was in bed, so I went down to Claude Morgan's and

I was so tired that I fell asleep milking a cow and woke up when she kicked

he said he would come with me. Mother made some hot drinks with ginger and whiskey for the cows. We got some boards, got some ropes and took the car out to Sudbury to see what was wrong. So off we set. The first cow was down in someone's garden. The next cow had slipped down right in front of the cemetery. The men had to go with the others, so they'd had to keep going. The only thing that they could do was to leave those that couldn't stand. They drove them down Sand Hill into Sudbury and herded them into the butcher's yard. The butcher said that was all right, but they had to stay in there for two weeks, before the weather gave up. We had to send hay and straw down there every day, we had to feed and water them. Anyway, after we'd seen to the men and got the rest safe, we all went back to the one at the cemetery. Claude Morgan was driving the car and his Aunt lived somewhere near and she bought out some tea. This was about 10 o'clock at night. We didn't know where to get a truck, or something to move this cow. If we could get her on something, we could get her off the road. We went to the pub called The Maldon Grey and we borrowed a

Muriel Rainsford's father and Studebaker.
Courtesy of Elizabeth Gardiner

Claude and Vera Morgan when they kept the Bear at Sudbury

pony dray that was used to put pigs in really. We then put ropes underneath this cow and bodily lifted her into that, but we'd got no pony in this dray. We managed to push this dray along with some of the men in the shafts, some of them at the back with the cow in and there's a little hill, before you turn down to The Maldon Grey. Well, when we went down this hill, that took charge, the trap and I don't know how we managed to stop it. We got down the hill to The Maldon Grey and unloaded the cow into a box down there. She eventually died - died of a broken back. Then we proceeded back to Cundy's Gardens. When you get to Cundy's Gardens, there is a turning where that bungalow is and you can go right across the fields and down to a Rectory. We'd got plenty of ropes, so we took a gate off the hinges. There was snow then about a foot deep. We rolled the old cow over onto the gate, then we tied the gate onto the back of the car, with the old cow's legs laid over the side of this old gate. One of the men got on her head and held her head down. We towed the gate right across the parkland to the house. We told the Parson the cow had gone down in the road and we put her in his yard, in a box in his yard. We eventually got her home days later, she was all right and she hadn't been home very long before she calved, she was a red cow calf. I never go past that gateway without thinking of that, but we lost the other poor old cow. They just couldn't stand, poor dears, in the unexpected snow. I do not know what I would have done without Claude Morgan's help. The old man put the kibosh on my relationship with him and he married someone else. He later came back to take The Bear in Sudbury.

I used to help to milk the cows then. We got this old cowman and the cows all tied up in the barn. We had room for 10 cows. Instead of milking them and then putting another 10 in, we used to milk them where they stood, so there were two lots of cows in the middle of the barn. The cowman's name was Sam and we all used to have to wear white milking aprons. There was water and a clean towel in the barn and you had to wash your hands after milking each cow. This old man was sitting beside the cow milking and I was doing the same thing on the other side and all of a sudden he spat. I thought to myself, dirty old man. What a nice how-do-you-do if it had gone in the pail. I never drank no more milk after that, it put me off milk for good and I don't drink it now.

After that we had a cowman called Cue Hughes. My father used to say: "How are the cows milking, Cue?", "Oh we're up on the milk, but Gambler's ill", or something like that, and he seemed to like telling you all the good news he could find. About this time we suddenly had a notice from the Co-op in Claydon, where we sold the milk to, that the milk had been watered. We could not think how possibly water could have got in. For weeks they rejected the milk and we could not understand it. We were getting no money at all, but it kept going on. The old man tried everything to find out. He tried locking the milk can to see if some had been taken out, he tried everything you could think of. In the dairy the milk used to run through a cooling freezer thing, we tested that. We tested everything we could think of, but we couldn't find what the trouble was and the old man said to me: "Well you'll have to stop with him, go where Cue goes". When I found out I couldn't believe it and do you know how I detected it? One morning he had to go to the house with a pail of milk, he'd taken four pails of milk into the house and

Driving Dad's Studebaker which I decarbonised several times

he came back to start milking another cow. Well I knew he'd taken all his milk he had got into the house. Then he sat down to milk his cows and I was milking cows further up the other side, and as he started to milk this cow, I heard the noise it made in the bucket. The noise not of the milk hitting the bottom of the pail, but hitting water, so I got up and had a look. He didn't know what to say, I looked in his pail and saw water in his pail. I said, "Why did you do it? It's cost us pounds and pounds and pounds," but he couldn't say anything. He just seemed to want to try and please us by making more milk but it cost us money we simply had not got.

My father also hired Mrs Mounsey's Park at Dedham for the horses and they had to walk from our place to Dedham on the road. We had to bring back a chestnut mare who never had a name. We had had her for about 15 or 16 year, she was a lot of trouble, she'd never been broken, never had a head collar on her. We were short of feed so we took a lot of horses to this Mrs Mounsey's at Dedham Park to be turned out. We took them over in two different lots, the carthorses and hunter colts all used to run together along the road. Sometimes there'd be someone in front sometimes not. There'd be two of us, me and Harry Tricker. I thought it's a long way to walk from Boxford to Dedham. I was leading a 2-year-old colt up Sand Hill at Boxford which had high banks on either side. The colt had a halter on so I drew it up beside the bank and I nipped on its back. It had never had anyone on it before, so it was a bit of a chance. I thought if it runs away, it will run up hill and I'll be able to pull it up. I got on its back and it walked with me like that all the way on his back to Dedham, 10 or 11 miles. When we went to take some of these horses home we brought the chestnut mare away. This mare was unbroken, she was always a lot of trouble and went crazy. If you take a horse like that away from the others they keep on hummering and she kept hummering back. She'd never had a bit in her mouth so you could only lead her. Anyway she kept rearing up but she reared up once too often. She reared up and went over backwards and she cut that little tiny knob on the top of her head right between the ears and that bled - it poured off her. That stopped her chatting in church. She just put her head down and the blood poured and poured. We did not know how to stop the bleeding, we tried everything we could think of, covered it with rags and all sorts. She just stood with her head down and let the blood run out of her. Then I remember something that Lazzie Pattle had told me - a cobweb. If you put a cobweb over it, that will stop the bleeding. We found a cobweb in the hedgerow, kept it intact with two hands and put that on it, we didn't have to lose much time either, but it made the blood clot and it stopped the bleeding and we walked her home. She was no trouble to walk home, poor old thing.

Chapter 13

I be a lad from Bungay Town and they call I Bungay Roger
The axed I o'r and o'r again if I would be a soldier
They axed I o'r and o'r again if I would take the shilling
Till up jumped I cor b..... I cried to show em I be willing
With a fol rol, fol the rol the day for the rol the day till I get home

Now they marched I into a dining hall as hungry as a hunter
the orderly officer he come in have you any complaints sir?
Then up jumped one and shouts out loud
My kippers only got one eye sir
I were young so I was last two buns and a dirty tater
With a fol rol, fol the rol the day For the rol the day till I get home

They marched I into a barrack square to do I's duty manuel
They bu.... I here and they bu..... there doing I's duty manuel
First eyes right then eyes left cor blast ye keep yer head up
And if I dare to say one word there'll bl.... I in the lock up
With a fol rol, fol the rol the day For the rol the day till I get home

Now I wish I were back home again following the bl... old plough sir
I wish I were back home again milking the bu... old cow sir
I wish I were back home again with plenty beef and mutton
With a rusty old fork and a bl... old knife cor blast e wouldn't I cut un
With a fol rol, fol the rol the day For the rol the day till I get home

Tickles learned this off Roly Fletcher down the White Hart.

We couldn't buy anything, we couldn't pay for anything we were as poor as church mice. We hadn't got enough to buy a penny stamp, not one iota. It was no good thinking that when you threshed a stack out you could sell the corn. Just as likely Wilson the corn merchant would hear that you were threshing and he'd send his wagons up for the corn because we were up to our neck in hock with him. We were well in his ribs. The Bailiffs came up and put stickers on the furniture and you had to sit and eat at a table and chairs with Bailiff's stickers on saying that if such and such money for the rates had not been paid within so many days they'd be taken away and sold.

If you hadn't got anything then you were lucky because you hadn't got to worry about it for sooner or later you'd lose it. We were getting in Bert Cook's ribs down the road, he was in the butcher's shop. We were well in his debt, I've forgotten how much we owed him. We were in everybody's debt and they wouldn't take the milk. No, not take the milk on the railway unless you paid for it before it went so if you hadn't got the cash to send it, they wouldn't take it. They didn't have accounts for that then. Things were so bad. I used to have a hole in my Wellingtons where the water used to run in and I used to have wet feet all day long. Things were so bad I couldn't afford to buy any more. I had no money off the old man. You had to wear boots, it went half way up your legs, the mud cause the yards were so out of condition.

I couldn't stick it any longer so I said I'm going to London to learn hairdressing. I asked my father for money to learn hairdressing because I was so fed up 'cause I had to look after these cows. He owed me no end. He said: "No daughter of

Two bailiff receipts for the rates that I paid

mine is going to be a barber. I'm not going to let you have any money". So I never had any but I'd saved every penny I had had then. I never spent one penny 'till I had enough money to go to London to learn hairdressing. I'd got about half what I wanted so I thought I'll go. He said: "Where did you get the money from?" I said: "I saved it, I saved all my money, every penny I could get hold of. I'm going to stay in a hostel". "You're not going to stay in a hostel, you will stay with somebody I know, a friend of mine. No daughter of mine is staying in London in a hostel", so that was that. I went up to London and stayed with Dad's friends, the Ninehams, and I went to see Madam Barry in Sloane Street, Knightbridge to learn hairdressing for three months. I don't remember how much it was, but it was a lot of money. I'd only saved ten or eleven pounds and I only had enough money to pay for 6 weeks not three months. I told her I lived on a farm and I was not sure if I would like it so I told her I would like to go for six weeks to see if I liked it, and Madam Barry let me go.

When I left to go to London hairdressing Dad took me to the station. I had two big heavy bags. When we got to the station I got out and he just drove off. He did not even say goodbye or help me with the bags. He then wrote to me in London to say he hoped I would die, and he never wanted to see me again. I used to write home to Mother and when he heard that I was getting on well and was starting to make money, his attitude changed and he would write such loving letters now. Then, when I'd been there a week or two I wanted to go home for the weekend. There was a train strike on but a student got on the train and drove the train from Liverpool

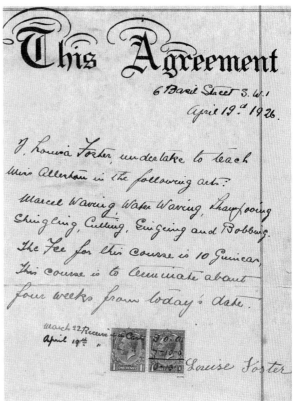

Street to Colchester. He was alright but he used to stop a bit too far out of the station and at another station he had a job to make the train go. It was a plucky thing to do. That was the first train strike, I believe.

Anyway, I went down to London and I got all my tools and I'm learning hairdressing. I hadn't been there only three days before I had to roll people's hair in the shop and put in waves and I'd never even seen a pair of tongs before. There was a woman there, she was nasty to me because I could get on so well. She'd say: "It's not fair, I've got three children to keep, why should you come in here and work straight away". Next thing I done was trimming. I had about a week more to go and I knew I was all right because they sent me over to another shop in Chelsea where they had got a hairdressing place. There were a whole load of girls learning, but they picked on me to work in the hairdressing salon. So I went over and worked there for a week. I thought if I'm good enough to work in their hairdressing salon and people are paying for it, I'm going to have to get a job. The

On my favourite Nabs, I could do anything with her

Manager said: "I don't want you to back into training school, there's no need for that, you've been in training school for so long, we've got another shop at Chelsea and I think the woman is doing me. Will you go over there?" So I went over there and he said: "You tell me if you think she's doing me or if there isn't the trade there" I went over there for a week, then I went home the next weekend having made an appointment at Woottens in Ipswich. Wootten said: "Where are you learning?" When I told them Madam Barry's in Sloane Street, Knightsbridge the man said: "I know it, it's a very good school". So he offered me a job at his Felixstowe shop to start in about a month's time when the season picked up. So I went down to Felixstowe and started at two pounds ten shillings a week after I'd only been learning the trade for 6 weeks and I'd only been getting £1 a week on the farm from the old man and that's if he paid me.

It was the 5th or 6th March 1926 when I went up to London and got that letter from Dad almost immediately telling me he'd hope I'd die because I'd left him. I didn't reply to him, but I wrote to Mother and I didn't stay with his friends at first, the

Pea House Farm. Boxford

Sunday evening

My Dear Ruby

Just a few lines wondering what you have been doing this Cold day. We have been round the fire all day as it is very Cold down here and I wanted a rest. I took Ed & Phil to Somer Dance last evening, there was not many people there, a poor Dance.

I am going to the 2nd 7 to 9 Races at Sayer on Tuesday next. Mr Bullock and Chas Raynham are going with me. I think I shall get out of Farming. I am sick of it.

I should like about a 50 acre Farm, near a Station on the main line about an hour from London just so that we had a Country home and could keep a Hunter or two and I should like a business in London or something of interest up there.

I shall not stop here when Ivna has finished School, I don't want such a lot of land, it is too much worry, 100 acres and half of it or more grass and a good house to what I shall look out for about 50 miles from London. Farming will get worse in this Country, we are flooded with foreign meat. To day it is 2d a pound cheaper. Mrs Letts asked me about you I told her all.

Your Dogs are quite alright they look well.

We have been having Hymns this evening 1½ hours of it.

Mrs Philo, (Ethel) is coming down this Easter, Her Husband works in Selfridges and they live quite near your Shop. At least I think so about 3d Bus Ride I think this is all my news. Write and tell us all news. Your Loving Dad
X.X.X.X.X.X.X.X.X.X.X
X

163

1. Have you entered the Colt in the Wickhambrook show?

2. If you cannot feed it send it back here you will never sell it you have been well advised not to.

3. — You are the sole cause of your Mother leaving her home. and under such circumstances she cannot claim one penny of me for maintenance. and what it more I will not pay her even to keep away. you have stole £5–14–0 in Mr Daking's Cheque Sold my Calves and Kept the money and you have

and you have obtained £4–10–0 of Mr Stanley Fairweather by False Pretence. He owes me this money for my Bull not you and you have no right to go to him and get this money without my permission especially after you have left here. You will hang about Botford until I have you arrested you are asking for it. You lied to Mr Daking. you told him you paid his Cheque into my account which was a lie. You cashed the Cheque and Kept the £5–10–0 and now you have been to Mr Fairweather unknown to me and asked him for money which he owes me. £4–10–0 and Kept it. The Colt you stole from here is Crabtrees no me dare buy it: it is stolen property. You will be in a muddle shortly, you must get your two dogs away from here to day

(margin) I will not have them here any longer

Nineham's. He didn't like that. Anyway on Sunday evening, 15th, he wrote to me still moaning and telling me that I was after Claude Morgan. He couldn't' seem to get Morgan out of his head. Anyway I still kept writing to Mother. Within a few days I had had another letter from him saying that 'We are very, very pleased to hear that you are getting on so well' telling me how much he loved me and then again on the 26th March. On 30th Dad knew the Nineham's because Nellie Nineham had lived in Bures and they now lived at 23 Castle Road, Stamford Hill. I had to get a bus from there to Finsbury Park, then a tube to Kensington.

While I was away at Felixstowe, Mother was so short of money she broke open my money box and they took the money out - they took the five shilling pieces and my sovereign. My old man was a dirty old bugger, he made my Mother do the dirty work. Mother had to go in the bank and pay in over the counter and she told the Bank Manager that she had had to break open the money box to get the money. There were high steps up to the bank. Mother came down off those steps and fell down and cut her head open and was taken to hospital. They sent a

164

telegram 'Come at once, Mother in hospital', I asked the old fellow in charge at Felixstowe "Can I go?" and he said: "Yes, get back as soon as you can". So I could go to see Mother then and I hurried to get home. Mother was crying, she said: "I had to open your money box. It worried me so much that I fell down". She was all right and I was back again the next day at my job. I told my Mother not to worry about it, but the old man was always after it. The first week's wages that I took at Felixstowe, I wrapped it up in paper and put it in the post and sent her, but of course that didn't last long. Then the old man said: "Will you come home? You must come home, pack in your job and come and drive the tractor. I've no one else to do it". So I went back and at Fudges, the farm where we used to grow the sugar beet, I ploughed that whole farm up. I told him I wanted to go back to my job again when I'd finished. He said: "Oh no, no, no... you've got to keep on what you're doing. I want you here". He promised me £1.00 a week and my keep, that's what he promised me sixpence an hour, but he never gave it to me. I never got it.

The first week I was home, he gave me the job of paying the men. He gave me a cheque to pay the men and when it came to paying out I hadn't got enough left over to pay myself a £1.00 a week. So the next week he gave me the money to pay them, I made sure of my £2.00, (that was a pound for that week and a pound for the week before) I took it out first. Later he sat down at the dinner table with a list, so much for Harry, so much for so and so, £2.00 for Ruby. "£2.00, What's that £2.00 for?"
I said: "Well you promised me £1.00 a week, I didn't have my £1.00 last week, so it's £2.00 this week". He picked up the bacon dish off the table, the big one with a well in it, I sat at the table, and he threw it at me and I ducked and it went in the wall and it cut a groove out the wall. I got up and got outside, that was the only thing I could do to get away from him. He said: "Fancy thinking of taking the money, when you know how hard up I am". I said: "Yes, but you promised it and I left my job to do it". Anyway I got hold of my £2.00 and I flung it at him and I said: "There's your £2.00, I'll never ask you for another penny as long as I live". I moved out the way, else I'd have got a hiding after another row and I cleared off down to Boxford.

I then bought the Hairdressers Journal and I saw a job going down in Guildford, Surrey, an all round hand, a manageress for a hairdressing shop in Guildford, so I wrote for it. I told them where I had been employed, all that sort of thing. They wrote back and they engaged me. Four pounds a week spending wages and 2/6 in the pound commission and tips as well. Well I met all types of people down there, people who had been out on the heath riding all morning. They used to come in and talk about horses and I used to say: "Oh I know, did you have so and so?" and they would say: "How do you know". So I said: "Well I can ride" and they would be really surprised and want to talk and they would ask for me and come in specifically to talk horses. It was such a good job. No one was earning £4.00 a week, it was terrific. Hairdressing and perming was the modern thing and there was a big demand for anyone with any skill. Edna was still at school and she was going to be a shorthand typist for Twenty Five bob a week. When I went down to manage the saloon, Dad then decided he would pay for Edna to learn hairdressing and she went and lived with Aunty Lou in London.

The window that Dad threw his dinner through

The landlady at Guildford was very kind to me, I had a bed-sitting room and my meals, thirty shillings a week, that was sort of tops then, that was a lot of money. They lived in the basement and had a window that backed out onto the garden and I went down there and I had my meals with them, I didn't eat in my room. I'd had the job for 4 weeks, then I got a letter from Dad, saying 'Come home and help me. Don't you think you ought to come home and help me. I want to get this done and that done.'

I never took no notice of it. Then along came a letter from Mother - I'm staying at Uncle Frank's, your Dad's thrown me out. Don't you think even though you've got a good job and you're earning good money, for the sake of your family don't you think you ought to come home. - I got in touch with Mother and told her I had received a telegram from Dad telling me to come home and get things squared up. The lady in charge told me to take a week off. So I had a week off from there to go home because Dad had said he wouldn't have Mother back unless she took me back and get straightened up. I'd ploughed up his land for him, now he wanted it drilled, but I went back. I went home. Mother was staying with Uncle Frank, Frank Pettit at Mount Farm, Bures. She had no money and couldn't carry on like that. The old man would pay nothing so she wanted to go to court so I borrowed a motorbike. Tom Skinner was a chap who weighed twenty stone and Triumph built a motor bike especially for him, he was a heavy weight, then he sold it and Ted Triton bought it. When I sat on the seat I couldn't reach the ground, so I always had to pull up on a bank. I had a carrier on the back and Mother got on, I took her to Colchester on it. They awarded her so much money.

I went home again in the October and Mother was still with Uncle Frank. Before I went home the old man had advertised for a housekeeper and he interviewed the housekeeper. He rang me up and said go down to Hadleigh station and pick her up and not being able to say no, I picked her up and dropped her off at the farm. Next morning one of the men bought a note down which said, please come and take me away. I'm not going to put up with your father's treatment.

I had only been in Guildford about a month, but I had to write to them to say I couldn't go back again. They wrote back saying they would wait for me. Would I please go back. I packed all my things ready, ready to go as I thought things were all right then, but nobody would take me to the station to go. Mother begged me not to go as he was going to turn her out again. He swore at Mother saying: "That bloody Ruby, she's only thinking about herself" and all that sort of thing and made Mother's life a misery. It was November, I had everything packed, and I was thrilled to be going back. Mother was upset 'cause I was going, and she would have to go too. The old man said he'd throw her out again so I said to my Mother: "I won't go back" and I didn't go back to Guildford. I saw how he treated Mother, how rotten he was to her, because of me going back, so I wrote and told them I was ever so sorry, but I couldn't make it.

He turned Edna out too, she went over to Mrs Hills. He wouldn't have anyone in the house except Sibyl. Edna never went home again, she went to Hadleigh and she stayed with her future sister-in-law. I wanted desperately to go back to Guildford. Mother kept begging me not to go and the old man kept putting on her, but I said "I'll never leave you no more, I shan't go". When I came home from Guildford I had saved £16.00, that was a lot of money. I was so afraid of losing it. I hadn't been home long before I didn't have any left. Dad kept saying: "Didn't you save any money?".

Amy Peak, the midwife who was Mother's friend and Inspector Peak's mother, was so busy she couldn't go out to get her hair cut, so she asked: "Could you cut it Ruby?" so I cut it for her. She said: "How much?" I didn't like to charge her, so she gave me some cigarettes. Next thing is she said: "Would you go and do Mrs So and So's", so I used to go out in the evenings. I only used to charge a shilling for a haircut and one and six for a wave. Some nights I might only earn five bob another night I might earn six or more. I would start work on the farm at 7 o'clock in the morning until 5 o'clock at night, Dad was supposed to pay me £1 a week and my keep. He never paid me. I used to go hairdressing at night time and then I used to give Mother ten shillings out of what I earned during the week towards my keep. I used to work all day for nothing and then give Mother ten shillings out of what I earned in the evening. Sometimes I did not get home until eleven at night and Dad would want to know where I had been, but if I hadn't been out hairdressing those nights, they'd have had nothing, nothing, nothing at all. If I had a late night and wanted a little lay in - no way. He'd get out of his bed to get me up then go back to bed again.

So I was back on the farm working as normal, but anything would suddenly upset the old man. He'd lose his temper in a flash and throw anything that he could lay his hands on. He had thrown something once through the window in the big kitchen at his father and had taken the centre bars out. They couldn't afford to have that replaced properly, so to this day there is one big pane of glass where there should be four small ones. But if you could get out of the way for a day or two, until he cooled down, you could go back and he'd be just as likely be as right as a mailer.

We hadn't any money and could sell nothing and the old man was going berserk. He had some wheat he wanted sold one day so he said: "Take a sample of that 40 ton of wheat and go down to Dan Alderton's at Hadleigh and sell it to him or Wilson". Dan Alderton would help and used to buy it off me and get me out of trouble. I was sleeping with Edna then in the front bedroom, we had a wardrobe with all mixed clothes hanging in. Anyway I went down there with a sample, but he was full up, he couldn't take any more in, so I left him and went up to Mr Wilson at the Station to sell it to them, but they didn't want any more either - they couldn't sell it. You could hardly give it away. Anyway I couldn't sell it to anyone else, so I'm starting to go home. I was longer than I should have been because I'd been to Wilson's as well. On the way home I went round to see Mr Mason, he was always very nice to me. He said: "What are you selling now dear?" I told him and that every where was full up. "How much

Board Lodging Etc
Stabling Straw
Chaff - Corn Etc

						August 1931			
						Rent for charge	2	0	0
						Rent for Claud & Harry	1	16	
I had off Dad.						Wages drilling		10	
						Wages next week		12	6
Mr Wilsons cheque	10	0	0			Rent Mrs for Coal		10	
Mr Lee dentist		5	0			Towards Rates		5	
Feb 29th 1932 Cheque on account	10	0	0			Cyril Rice		6	
						Grocries		3	5
June 15th 1932 On account from Sale of Cow Calleston	5	0	0			Claude		10	
						Hair Dye		3	9
						Oil & Bike		3	3
Jan 30 1932 off account Kimball	1					Oil		3	0
						Phone calls			4
						fares to Sudbry twice		2	6
						Rent		10	
	✓					Dad Saturday		3	
							7	18	9
						Mrs Hancock	5	0	0
						Mr King Rates	10	7	0
						Grocries		1	2
							23	6	11

We had no money, I leant him all I could and this is shown in the loan book of money that he owed me

170

Carried forward	23 - 6 - 11	
bacc to Sudbury	12	0
Bovril & Groceries	3	0
Oil	3	0
Claxso	2	6
Dad Friday evening	2	0
Cue's Wages	1	13	9
Lu	1	14	9
Blanda	1	10	0
W. Kemballe Sale	1	10	0
Sent to pay Rennie Rice	18	0
Car to Sudbury D	4	0
Mrs Stray	3	6
Phone Calls	1	10
Sudbury fare	1	0
Rocks	1	1
Rent to pay Rennie alcoo	10	0
25½ hours drilling on Browns	12	9
Last Bit of Interest to him	4	0	0
£ 37 - 5 - 1		

Carried forward	37	5	1
Mr Rose Pigeon money	1 - 0	0
Mr Clarke Green etc	2	1
Rent for Rennie on Saturday	2	0
" towards Groceries	1	6
1 cwt Coal Monday	2	3
Stamps		4
Tiib Bichines		6
Took out of Purse	3	0
Groceries		10
Blacksmith	1	3
Groceries + Phone	4	4
Rent to go to Boxford	1 - 6
B. Dance Ticket	7	6
Car ride	2	0
Spent at Dance	5	0
39 - 19 - 2		
Ipswich with Dad	3 - 0
Rent for Paraffin	1 - 0
40 - 3 - 2		
40 - 3 - 2		

Carried forward	40 3 2
Borrowed for Wages (Ca)	5 - 0 - 0
mar 5th from £10 cheque	

= £ 15 - 14 - 2

Keep paid for Ruby, Mar 2
to Dec 31st 1934

Sow Ruby
£ 19 - 14 - 0 only
Charles Allerton
Jan 4th 1935

Brought Forward	19	14	.
Carpet	4	
	23	14	.
Less 73 - 0 - 0 Cheque	
" Mares Keep to Sept 15 1935	
5 - 10 - 0	
8 - 10 - 0	8	10	.
£ 15	4	.
On Sept 15th 1935	
Borrowed for Harveys Wages	11	.
Chas Allerton £ 26	4	.

have you got?" he said "I'll try and find room for some more." So I got the sample out to show him. Dad had told me not to take less than so and so. When he said he could do with some, I put the price up. What ever Dad had said I put about two shillings a comb on it. He said: "I'll take it". I was really pleased so I then went on home.

When I got home Mum met me and she said: "I thought you'd have been home before this". I said: "I know, but I couldn't sell it to Alderton then I went to Mr Wilson and he didn't want it, so I went to see Mr Mason". She said: "You're too late, do you know what he's done? He's taken your photographs off the wall, one of you on a horse, from the dining room, and he's been upstairs and got your big photograph"- the one my Grandma Nen had done for Mother - he'd taken them down and cut the eyes out of them then taken them down the yard, got the paraffin can and set fire to them. Another time he went upstairs and went to my wardrobe. I was always making things, even when I was not living at home. He got my dresses out and slit them in two. Anyway I ran away to get out of his way 'cause you never knew what he'd do and I went up to our neighbours, the Kemball's who lived at The Cox Farm about a mile up the road towards Boxford.

Some of the cheques that Dad gave me. They were all unpresentable

I went down to Boxford and I got lodgings with Mrs Mabel Munson. Pot Munson she was called. The old girl drowned herself in the end, she put her head in the water butt, but that was way after I'd left. But when her son came home, I moved in with Mrs Goymer next door in Swan Street next to The Swan. She was the mailman's wife. The mailman used to collect the mail. He would leave Boxford at 8 o'clock every night and pick up all the letters and take them to Colchester. He would stay in Colchester and come back the next morning and would arrive about twenty past five with all the letters to be delivered in Boxford. He had a Ford van. He had a daughter Stella. After I had been there a few weeks I moved into a cottage at 2 Stone Street Road. It was one shilling and seven pence a week and I told Claude, who had then been staying at Mrs Rule's in Broad Street, next door to the Kembles. Mrs Rule said to Claude: "now that Ruby has got a cottage if you want to go you can". So I took Claude in and he lived with me.

John Goymer
the mailman

One night when I was there, I had some Carol Singers come to the door. They were boys from the village after a few pence and

Mrs Goymer
and I

I knew that one was Tom Skinner. I went upstairs with a bag of flour and gently dropped some out of the window on the boy Skinner. "Blast that snew" he said. So I dropped a bit more, then a whole lot more, on his head and he looked up and said: "That's yer b..... Ruby!". So I asked them in and gave 'em a mince pie each after that. I kept the cottage on even after I went back to the farm, I didn't want to lose it 'cause that was nothing to pay, the rent you see was so little and I knew I'd always have somewhere to go to, a bolt hole if there was any trouble. I kept it on for some time then Claude was getting married and he couldn't find a cottage in Boxford. He knew I'd got that cottage and said would I let him have that. I let him have it on the condition that when he didn't want it

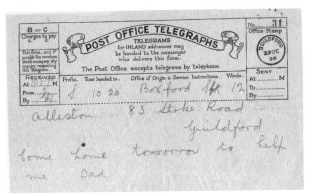

any longer I would have it back again. They lived there for several years and during that time the fireplace wore out and they had another fireplace put in. When they had that other fireplace put in - Claude's father-in-law Chief Inspector Saunders died. He had been Chief Inspector in the Police and they had the chance to move into Sudbury to the house that big house - that he owned. The Murrells in Melford Road. So they didn't want the cottage any more. Instead of giving me the cottage back as he promised he would do, he let Val Wymark have it, because Val Wymark was going to pay for the new stove they had put in. I never had my cottage back. Claude got married in 1934.

About the time I was living in Boxford, I was getting on real well doing dressmaking and hairdressing. Then one day I was walking down the street and I was about a foot off the pavement when suddenly, there was a chap at Edwardstone who used to take a boy to school and, as he worked for this man in Edwardstone he was allowed to drive his car. I saw him go by in this car, I thought he was going home. Suddenly he reversed down the street and reversed right over the top of me, knocked me down. It's a wonder he didn't kill me. In those days there used to be a carrier on the back of a Morris 8. I was caught on the end of the carrier. He kept on going, he never stopped. My legs were all cut and covered in oil and grease where they hit the gearbox underneath. I said: "Didn't you know you ran me over?" He said: "Well I heard it hit something, but I didn't know what it was". My hands and arms were just about to give out 'cause I was holding onto the edge of this iron bar on the carrier. I got his name and address and the insurance people came to see me. I didn't know how long I would be laid up, I didn't know how to deal with them. I was laid up for a long time. Anyway they said would I take £30.00 to settle, and £3.00 for my coat. I thought I'd better take the money. Well my Father heard about it and the next thing was he wrote and asked if I would lend it to him to pay the rates. He'd been summoned for non payment and if he didn't pay the rates the bailiffs would come and take the furniture.

Dad said: "You won't get on the bus until you get into Boxford Street, but I shall get on by the Police Station, and when you get on in Boxford Street, please don't speak to me or take any notice of me and ride to Sudbury. When you get off at Sudbury you can give me the money so I can go and pay the rates." and that's what I did. He wouldn't let me speak to him all the way to Sudbury. He made out to everybody that I was a scapegoat and no good and he wouldn't like to let people think that he was borrowing money off me. I never got a penny of it back, ever and all the cheques he gave me. I never got a penny of those back. He tell me not to put them in the bank, because there wasn't any money, he'll tell me to hold onto them until there was some money in the bank. There never was enough in the bank for me to draw it.

He only paid me back £13.00, that's all he ever paid me in all my lifetime and that's because I was married to Arthur and he'd borrowed £13.00 in front of Arthur.

I was hairdressing and dressmaking and getting on like a house on fire. I did some dressmaking for the Hessies. The Hessies were retired and very well off, and lived at Edwardstone. One of the girls was going abroad and wanted some cotton frocks made, so I made her some. I never knew how much to charge them. The cook up at Hessies was a young girl and she was getting married and she asked me to make her wedding dress. I made a satin wedding dress and I lined it throughout and I charged her six shillings.

My cottage was 4 Stone Street and was right against the school, it was owned by someone from Twinstead. Reg Fletcher, who had worked for us, lived in one side and I lived in the other. Claude had the quinsies while he was at the cottage with me and Dr Everett came to see him. The cottage I was in had one downstairs room and a little tiny piece for a kitchen at the back which you could cook in, and out of that kitchen went the staircase, very much out of repair and with no carpet on. I remember the Doctor going up there to see Claude and saying you must keep changing his sheets. Claude was sweating all the time and I asked Edna if I could borrow some sheets but she was getting married and did not want to lend any.

On the opposite side of the road lived a man named Ruben Gunn; he never got married. His sister was married, she was a Mrs Hills and a very good looking woman. Anyway Ruben lived down there on his own and he never cut his finger nails; he let them grow and his fingernails were about two inches longer than his fingers. Next door to Ruben Gunn lived a family of Gants. During the First World War, father Gant had to go to the war and he was killed and he left a large family. The mother worked hard and she kept them very respectable, always well dressed. I used to like George best. When he was young he used to come rook scaring, scaring the rooks off the fields and my father used to send me to see he hadn't run home. There was Maggie and another girl, Vera. Ronnie Gant drove a lorry, then

176

he had to go into the army and was killed in the Second World War.

Then there was Mrs Mann who had two daughters and they both got pregnant at the same time. They weren't married and she said "They gals hev bin silly boys, bor. They gal's hev bin silly boys!"

Bloss Kingsbury was a big builder in Boxford and they'd been going for years and they had three sons, but we couldn't afford him. Tubby Rose was another little builder down there. One year they wanted something special to have at the fete, so they got Tubby Rose to make a life size catch 'em alive' mousetrap, big enough for a man to crawl in and they put a bar of chocolate in so that when it was touched, the trap went and you were caught. It was good so they got it down there at the fete and Tubby Rose had made this thing. Everyone tried to get the chocolate but they were all caught. Then Tubby Rose had a go and he got the chocolate alright. He was the only one who could work it. Every year they used to hold a fete, I used to look forward to that. They used to have a long wire fixed onto a tree that went right across the park and where it ended was in a lot of bags full of chaff for you to land in, to take the jar. You would hang on a thing with two handles on over the top of wire. To get up onto the wire you had to get onto a wagon, then onto some boxes, so you got right up high, then away you went. One of the farmers used to give a pig and you could 'bowl for a pig' as well, they always had that.

Red House Farm
Boxford. Suffolk.
Nov 9th 31

Ruby.

And I think you are well
named. I am writing this letter
to clear up everything between
you and I. for good, & for ever

In the 1st place you are no relation
to me what so ever,
I was dragged into marriage much
against my wish. and you
were born 3 months after marriage
Had I known what I afterwards
found out. you would have been
illegitimate if not some other man
would have been your Father,

But Fate dragged me into this awful
Marriage. I have done my best
to make the best of it. you have

II

after the age of 14th made my life and
home a Hell.
You were expelled from a Miss Bury's
private school at Hadleigh through
your Morals.
You went to business at Felixstowe
and were soon turned out of respectable
lodgins. Then you went to live in an
underground basement with an
Woman of the lowest type
You were Turned out of your home
here owing to your Moral Conduct
You were out all hours of the
night - and wanted to lay in bed
half the day.
You have been mixed up with 3 Three
Married men. Boreham, Morgan,
& Clarke. you have been out all
hours of the night with scores
of fellows of all classes.
Farm Labourers. oil rags.
Lorry Drivers, and servant Boys

Anyway I kept getting notes from Mother and there would be notes come down from Dad 'Would I go back up the farm.' I eventually got back up there again and I'm ploughing the land and that like and I kept asking for my money and the money back he owes me and I know I will never get any although he had given me an IOU on this mare Honor Bright. I never got any money for her either so after a time I said that I was going to sell her. The old man agreed but didn't like it. I told him I was going to contact Clark from Hundon who bought horses and Clark said that he'd come over.

He said: "I'll have a look at her, tell me how much you want for her". Mr Clark from Hundon was the one who I used to buy the straw off and had been over before to look at a colt. Dad was driving the tractor and I walked across the field and I said: "Dad, I want the money I lent you for Honor Bright, because I've bought Clarky over here to have a look at it". Clarky was stone deaf, he was in the war and was blown up or something. Dad went mad and was going to hit me, Clarky got in quick and knocked him down. I cleared off after that and so did Clarky.

I heard that the old man was huffing and puffing and fuming.

He was now saying dreadful things about me and this Mr Clark, a man years older than me and who I only knew because he came and bought our straw and also dealt in horses. Not only could the old man not stand being knocked over by old Clarky but he was writing letters round to everyone now. That was in November 1931. He wrote to me and said I wasn't his daughter and he wrote to Mr Clark. He had had so much of his own way at Aunt Sarah's when he was a boy and everything he wanted and he just could not deal with these things. He couldn't lose somehow.

He got Tickles to write me a letter saying how he had galloped my mare. Dirty trick wasn't it getting the boy Tickles to write. He knew that I would not be happy with how he was treating my horse. The next time I was up the farm I took Tickles down to Sudbury and I bought him a new suit and cap but he just wore it the same as he did his other clothes for messing about in. He'd never had anything new before and knew no better.

The old man made me responsible for everything. It didn't matter if it was the cows, the horses, the men or whatever, he laid in bed and said: "If I go broke, it's your fault". That's what he used to say to me. "If I go broke and we're out of this farm, it's your fault, and that was whether I

IV

Catling spouted about you and Claude Morgan and Borham. It was you who was at the bottom of your Mother taking me into Court to obtain a Seperation allowance. As Soon as No 4 was ready, you had your brother think but your oily Tongue cannot decive me. or your Cunning. You are the lowest down Rotter that I have ever had any thing to do with. and time will prove my words and I thank God that you are no relation of mine it was only my misfortune that I had to bring you up you Bastrdly Cad. Your heart is as black as hell and I hate you beyond words. I have destroy every picture in this house of you, and you shall never enter my Home again dead or alive
Yours Etc Charles Alleston

III

During the past two years you have been living in Boxford. You have had 4 homes. you are now in the 4th Why? Why did the three previous homes get sick of you. You have a soft oily mouth. but a tail hanger's to you.
I know what is going to happen to the 4th Place you are at. you cannot help it, Every one in Boxford Knows now what your trouble is, they believed your soft oily Tounge at first But Actions speak louder than Word. and You are now in your 4th Show "The Abode of Love".

When you were 15 years old you lied to your Mother about me. You did your utmost to turn her against me. You Told her about Doris Catling. Because Doris

Red House Farm
Boxford Suffolk,
Nov 7th 1931

Ruby.

What sort of a person do you call yourself. You bring two of your men in the field to me and clime round my tractor and tell me you are going to take my mare away. What do you think I am. Why didnt you do it? I am not afraid of your men You will never have a thing from here, There is nothing here yours. And if you dont send my Guns back I will make you. You are lowest rotten Cad of a Greek there is on Gods Earth. to only a few people know you, And the blackness of your heart

you are man mad, And you will come to the very lowest before you die You want a Cottage. What for? Every Sane person knows what for You Call a married man with Children my friend You are not respectable You are now in your 14th home in Boxford during the past two years. I realize that you are no relation to me. its all a rotten mistake. and my down fall.
I am Charles Allerton

was there or not. That used to worry me. He was a rotten old bugger. During the time I was back home, I used to go hairdressing in the evenings, Harry Tricker used to come in and go up the stairs - I don't know where he got the key from - but he used to go up the stairs and speak to the old man. He'd knock on the door and say: "Fine mornin', Sir." Dad would say: "Oh yes Harry". "Where are you going to get that money for the milk this morning? I need the money to pay for the milk to go on the railway. They won't take it without a cheque." Dad would reply: "Ruby was out working last night, she'll have some money." Harry used to come and knock on my door. "Ruby I want the money for the milk"; and so for peace and quiet I paid the money to put the milk on the rail.

I'd had this row and said I was going for good but he kept saying: "You'll come back, 'cause you've got that old horse down here". He got Harry Tricker to nail up the double doors on the box and put a padlock on it. He said: "If anyone comes into the yard after that horse, I shall lay them low. I'm taking my gun upstairs with me", he told Harry. I wanted to get my horse away.

Claude Morgan was working for Ellinger, driving the lorry and Ted Triton he was a mechanic and I asked them to help me get my horse away. Mr Ellinger said: "I'd like to be in this, too" I thought we don't want him he'd be sure to bugger it up, anyway he said he was coming.

We all went up there together one moonlight night about 12 o'clock. We went down the road, the four of us. I whistled my greyhounds, they came out and I put the leads on and gave them to Ted Triton to hold. In the yard, you came out of the cart lodge, down towards the horseboxes and you had to go through mucky water to get to them. The straw came up and floated on top of the water so it looked like a straw bed. It was one of those old yards where they stack all the muck in the middle, but the muck had all gone and it left a hollow where this filthy water hung about. We went over the little bridge into the stack yard and Claude Morgan got the poker, we went up to the horse box. I'd got a head collar. Claude prised the padlock off. I put the head collar on the mare and said: "Come on girl" and she walked out. We'd got a torch. I knew how to get through that horse yard by going round the side without going through that water. Claude followed me as I led the horse round, Ellinger came over the bridge, he was a bit behind us and did not follow our tracks. He had plus fours on and he went right in the water, right over these plus fours, he was wet through. Claude laughed. Then I took the filly - my Nabs - down the White Hart, but the next day a policeman came round. The police came down to me at the cottage and said: "There's a valuable filly been taken away from this farm". I said: "Well that's my filly. I can prove it" and I found the piece of paper I had for her, the one with love on (see page 106). They agreed Dad had not got a case against me so I kept it at The White Hart. That was the one I sold to Dad on 22nd June 1928. It was a 3-year-old. I used to take her along the road

> Red House Farm
> Boxford
> April 29" 1924
>
> My Dearest Ru,
>
> ++++ x x x x x x x x +x x x
>
> Peter has not got
> her fole yet but we
> are inspecting if
> ony day now. bab has
> been out on your
> mare to bay and he
> galloped her a mile
> round 20 acres. royal, is
> quite well. With
> love from Tick. x x +x x x xx
> x x x x x x x x x x x xx xx x x xx x x x

every day and she used to eat the grass off the road side and when she'd had a belly full, I used to take her home back to The White Hart. Then I'd be hairdressing and dressmaking at other times and earning a living that way.

So I continued down in Boxford and he kept writing notes but the next things I knew was I got another letter from Mother and he'd turned her out again. He had copperplate hand-writing and was now sending notes to everyone he could think of even mother's solicitor and the vicar about me. He always was articulate. Even in the bad times he always managed to dress well when he was out. He always wore a fancy waistcoat. Mother knitted him yellow ones and they all had a fox or hound's head buttons. At market he wore a box cloth long check jacket and only did the top button up so that you could see his watch chain. When he knew that we could dye hair we had to do this - jet black with a centre parting. That's what the Inecto is for on his account - it's the cost of his hair dye.

Anyway I had the cottage so I told Mother that I would go back. I met Mother in Sudbury - she came by train from Bures. We came home on the bus from Boxford and we walked up the road hand in hand together. He said he wouldn't have Mother home unless she brought me with her. He walked up to the front gate delighted to meet us.

182

That's how I came to go back up there and Claude got the cottage. I said to Mother: "I'll never leave you!"

Even in the times when Mother was away he kept sending me notes down in Boxford and expecting me to go up and clean the house for the new housekeeper or sent notes by Harry to send him more money for the milk to go on the train. Why I did it I just cannot think.

The old man tried to make out that I had carried on with Claude Morgan, a married man, and others and that I had bad morals and was expelled from Miss Byer's private school in Hadleigh. Well that wasn't true. I'll tell you what happened. One day all us children were cycling home from Hadleigh and there were several others, we were going up the hill and they were saying if you look over that door you can see the old cow having a calf - nobody knew about that sort of thing - and saying about how calves and children came out of tummies. The next thing is they had me on the carpet. I'm leaving there that term to go to Sudbury. I was 11 or 12. Miss Byers said you've been talking about things you ought not to talk about. I said: "I haven't". She said: "Yes you have, on the way back home, you were discussing things you never ought to talk about, why have you done this?" She made me feel so bad, she made me cry. I still maintained that I hadn't. She picked on me 'cause I came from the smallest family. Well nothing happened, but she wrote to Mother to say I'd been talking about things I ought not to have done. I was not expelled, but Mother would not send me back to school, because I was innocent and there was only about a week to go to the end of term and then I would be starting a new school at Sudbury in any case, but the old man would swear black was white if he felt like it.

Even in the bad times Dad always seemed to dress well to go out

He brought this all up later and so he did when I sold the bull and kept the money. He knew I'd kept it because he hadn't paid me

Monday evening

Dear Ru. We have just received your letter. And we are very very pleased to hear you are getting on so well. I knew you would. I told you how to go on, be interested, keen to learn. Say you like the business. Then when your fortnight is up. Say you must go home to see your people. They will be after you if you look like work and can do the job well.

I think we can talk better than we can write; You must learn the business well I should think the Lady you mention is good business, is she a right good allround hand? no doubt if you can get with her later you will have some good experience

Your Dogs are quite well. I have upset Harry Tucker he has gone home ill again he is worthless with stock I am on their track.

I shall have a small farm near some Town where we can have some Hunters. and a good time.

I am finished with Boxford. I love my old Ru. Dear old Ru. God Bless you, Yours truly Dad
x x x x x x x
x x x x x x
x x x x x
x x x
x x
x special

and I told him so, but he tried to make out I sold it, took the bull to a dealer Mr Fairweather of Bildeston and when he paid me the five pounds for it I told the old man that I was keeping it in lieu. He also tried to make out that I stole the one pound that Jack Dakin gave me everytime that I sold him calves but that was just luck money. The tip you always give someone back when you buy cattle from them. It was my perks and I kept it.

One day there were some races and Charlie Raynham had got a taxi and there were two or three of them going. They asked Dad to go with them. He said: "Have you got any money Ru?" I said: "I'm down to my last pound Dad, my last pound". Oh he started off again, he went and got in the car at the farm gate. I picked up my pound and ran through the garden and stopped the car, when it got to the white gates and gave him my pound.

One time I ran to get away from the old man, I was down in the village and I bumped into Claude Morgan's wife and she said: "I have a spare bedroom, come in with us". I was only there a couple of days, but the next morning because I hadn't gone back home he sent two men down with all the greyhounds. This was the time when he wrote to Claude Morgan saying that I was carrying on with him. There was a litter of 5 or 6 puppies and three grown greyhounds. Two of them I'd won stakes with. I said: "Whatever can I do?" I was nearly out of my mind. Claude's wife said: "I'll tell Claude that you're coming", Claude said: "There's only one place they can go. You can put them in the yard". They had to go into the coal house. The next morning I had to pocket my pride and take them back. I had to go back to the farm. Then he wrote me a letter to say I'd been seen kissing and cuddling Claude. I thought it was Mrs Grimwood opposite who had stirred it up. I hated her after that. He said it was her, of course but it wasn't her, it was Charlie Rainham. All the time Charlie Rainham was at the back of all this. He was friendly with Dad and to keep in with Dad he knew the old man and I didn't get on together. He was two-faced. He used to be ever so nice to my face. Claude said: "Let me keep a copy of that letter".

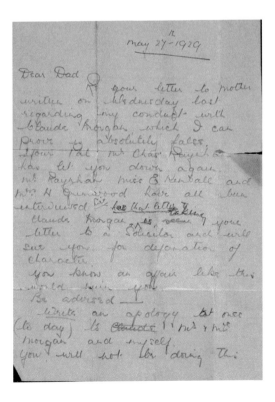

185

In 1930 the old man said that he was going to let Common Meadow and the Hollies back meadow. So I said can I have it and he agreed to let it to me for £14 a year and I had to pay 6 months in advance. I paid him as he asked then when I went to put the horses out there he would not let me have it, and I never got my money back. All he wanted was to get some more money out of me and that's how he got the money you see because I had to pay some of it in advance.

Groton Place was the home of Mr William Kemble - he was the brother of Charles Kemble of Boxford. When he died the place was sold and some Americans bought it. This young couple arrived from America. Harry Tricker our foreman went to live up the road in one of the cottages called 'The Oblong' and next door to him was empty. When Dad was down in The Fleece one day, these Americans who were staying there asked him if he would let the cottage to them. Dad said yes. When the Americans had got Groton Place ready, they moved in. Of course they had got friendly with Harry living next door to them and they asked him to go and live there with them and he did. He went to work there. The Americans went back to America a lot and Harry Tricker and his wife and family went and lived in Groton Place, in the house itself. One night there was a knock on the door and Harry Tricker stood there and said: "Is your Dad there Ru? I want to speak to him".

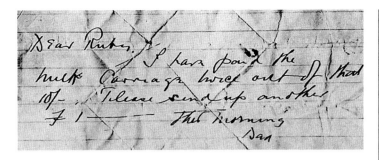

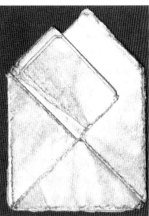

When he came in he said: "I left you Guv'nor, but can I come back? My wife is so unhappy". So Dad said: "Why, what's wrong?". "Well", he said: "In Groton Place every night time you can hear someone walk down the stairs, and when my wife puts the children to bed she leaves a lighted candle with them and somebody would come and put it out. It's definitely haunted and it's getting on our nerves and she wants to get out and there's a rattling of chains. If I can't get my wife out of there she'll go round the bend". Dad said: "Come on back Harry". So he came back and he moved back into The Oblong Cottage again.

Dad always folded these milk carriage notes like this

I remember I was riding Swannee one day and it was a little bit foggy, I was riding up towards home. It was a murky November day and I suddenly saw coming up the road a huge ball, like fluff - like a ball of tow. It was coming down the road- on the side of the road on the grass. It kept coming and coming. The old mare never saw it. There was a gateway on this side of the road and it stopped when it got to that gateway and sort of paused, then it went straight across the road right through the fence and across the fields.

Another time when the London cousins came down and stayed with us, we always used to go to church in the evenings. There was Ila, Mother's help and those three girls. We were all walking arm in arm along the road and suddenly Florrie, let go of my arm. I said: "Whatever did you do that for?" She said: "Well you saw that person wanted to pass, didn't you". I didn't see anybody, and there had been somebody pass between us, and I hadn't seen anything at all, and we turned round and there was no one there.

One night I'd been to Groton to Cora and Leonard Underwood's who farmed round at Groton Heath and when it was late and time to go home Leonard went to light the carbide lamp for me on the little put put bike. He put a match to my acetylene lamp on the motorbike. I had to go roundby Groton Wood to get home, then to Kersey Tye, then to The Four Cross Roads where Mary Towns' mother lived, then down that road and home. It was a moonlight night, I hadn't got a light on my motor bike because although they put a match to it and turned it on, it wouldn't light. So I said "I can see, it's a lovely night, so I'll go home without a light", but when I got to the old straw stack, where the fields are that used to belong to Mrs Hills and Charlie Bullock used to farm them for her, I was already scared because this was the spot where I had seen the woolly thing. When I got to the woolly, all of a sudden my light went on and I got the most brilliant light you ever saw in your life and I hadn't done anything to it. At the same time the stand at the back, where you pull your motor bike up on the stand, the stand dropped down. When that stand dropped down I daren't stop there. I rode on, and the stand kept clanking up and down all the way down the road until I got right down to where Jimmy Green lived. When

Wyn Saunders, who married Claude, sitting on Blossom

I got to this little group of houses I stopped. I thought I'll pull up I can't stand this clang, clang, clang. I kept my motor bike running and nipped round the back of my bike to pull the stand up, and the stand was already up!! I rode home, put the bike in the cart lodge and ran indoors terrified.

Edna had seen something up there too, she had seen a ball of wool up there, I also had seen it up at the same place. That came out of one side of the road, crossed the road and went in the other side. I was pedalling my bike along, it was a job to miss it, so after that we always called that area just the other side of where Jimmy Green lived, 'The Woolly.'

Kersey Street, Mrs Gages house where Harry Aggis used to have his Pork Butchers Shop is on the right

Chapter 14

The British Soldiers Grave
The battle it was over the stars were shining bright
The moon shone on the dying and the dead
Not a sound could be heard, but the song of wild birds
As they fluttered round the dying soldiers head.

And on the deck there lay one who nobly fought the day
His comrade true to him was standing by
But he with anguish side and to his comrade cried
And with a hand he wiped a tear away

Oh tell my dear old Mum that I'm not coming home
And take this parting gift she gave to me
For a locket stained with blood is all that she will have
Of a son that lies somewhere across the sea

And remind my sweetheart Annie of that fallen willow tree
Where we cut our names and hearts of love
And tell her not to cry, I'll meet her by and by
In that bright and better land that lies above

Then he whispered goodbye to his comrade so dear
His head upon his knapsack gently lay
If I'm spared to reach home, I'll tell 'em that you have gone
And lying in a British soldiers grave

I think that I got this off Reg Fletcher

Claude could be jealous when he was a young boy. One day when he was helping us load the harvest wagons and had a big load on, the men were saying: "Come on Claude, you can't load as well as your sister". You fling a rope over and tie it on the side, you see, then you slide down on that. I went down on the cart rope and Claude went down on the cart rope. He was doing the back and I was doing the front. When he got half way down the

Claude

load, he gave it such a pull to try and pull my load arse over head. I shouted: "Don't do that, you'll pull my load off". You see he was going down on my rope on the front. When he got down and he put his feet on the ground, he hit me with his fist right between the eyes. The chaps saw him do it. I'd never had a nose bleed before and that spurted with blood. I held my head down and he didn't know what to do. The chaps said to Claude: "You've done it now". Claude ran away and he went round Gypps Piece pond country. Anyway, it blacked both my eyes and one eye I couldn't see out of. Oscar Marten was there and Dolly Padlock. I went home and Dad and Mum were there and they said: "Oh my goodness, where is he?" I went and cleaned up my face, then I walked down to Gypps Piece and kept calling out: "Come on Claude, I'll forgive you" 'cause you see he wasn't going to come back.

When Claude left school in Sudbury, he worked at the farm. The old man kept cutting him down, he didn't want to pay him as much as he paid the men. Of course he lived in the house. I don't know what happened, but one night my Father wrote to Claude and told him he wasn't allowed in the house anymore. He'd been making eyes at the maid or something like that and my old man, he was priority number one in that field. Father was jealous so Claude had to go. He was only 17 and hadn't left school long. He went to Boxford. He picked up his things and went to Mrs Rule. She lived next door to the Kembles on the corner of Butchers Lane and Broad Street, opposite the White Hart yard. Then there was the lane, then there was a house, then another house, it was a big house where Mrs Rule lived. She took him in and he paid her £1 a week lodgings. He went up to see Mr Daking at his farm and he gave him a job there sugar beeting. When my father heard he was sugar beeting for Jack Daking he nearly went crazy. "My son going to work for another farmer and pulling sugar beet of all things. This cold winter day, when it's freezing". It was damned hard work knocking and topping sugar beet. You had to pull them out, pick them up and you chopped the top off and slung them in a heap. You had a sack tied round you with binder string but your hands got frozen. I think father was so ashamed - he wrote to Claude a four page letter. Later on he kicked Tickles out as well but Tickles went back.

Ted Triton was also lodging with Mrs Rule. Mrs Rule's husband had the village bus at this time. Dan'l Griggs used to drive for him and go round and deliver the coal off the back of this same lorry during the week. Claude thought more of Mrs Rule than he did of his own father. He used to go back there every birthday and took her some strawberries and cream. When she got old and couldn't get out, he still went to see her.

Jack Daking was at school with my father - he sat next to him. If we had any calves for sale Jack Daking would buy all our heifer calves. Whenever I went to see him, he knew what the old man was like and if I sold him some calves he always used to give me a pound. Claude went to work for Ellinger after that. The first man who had lorries round there was Peter Knott, Will Knott was his father, he was the transport bloke and he lived in Stoke, Claude went to work for him, driving a lorry. He had a Ford van, he would put a cattle top on the flat buck and he would transport cattle backwards and forwards to Ipswich. Claude worked for Barney Wyatt of Flowton when he came home from the war (1939-1945). Barney Wyatt was a cattle dealer, he had been to Ipswich Hospital for something. He was a big man and became quite famous for raising money for Hospital charities.

The story was that he stood on Ipswich Cornhill one day and had a raffle. He offered a prize 'worth a guinea'. When the winner got it he found that he'd only won a box of Beechams Pills. When he complained, Barney Wyatt showed him the lid where it was written 'worth a guinea a box'. Claude had been in the RAF during the war and had spent a lot of time in Africa with the Kikuyu tribe. After he left Barney Wyatt he started his own transport and had a garage in Sudbury.

At this time I had a cottage in the village, when Mrs Rule said to Claude: "Now that Ru has got a cottage, if you want to go you can" So Claude came to live with me. He used to have the small bedroom. He had to pay me something for being there so he used to pay me 7 shillings a week. For that I used to do all his washing and he had the bedroom at the back. I used to feed him Saturday, Sunday and made his sandwiches for the week. Claude was a good worker and a good boy but he would make up os many damned stories that were not true and you could not always believe him.

Chapter 15

In a rickety old cottage as ploughmen I dwell
With a family eight and my wife as well
I stick to my duty the whole of the day
Weather fine wet or cloudy I still peg away
Sometimes it is not but laugh it all
So hurrah for the ploughmen who live at Frog Hall

Arthur Baalam who Tev Partridge sent to help out sung this. He said it was about Frog Hall Layham and has lots of verses

One day when the old man had no one and badly needed a hand his friend Tev Partridge sent up Arthur Baalam, his horseman, to help. Arthur did his day's work and the old man said: "I'd like to give you a drink Arthur but I have not got a bean to my name".

Arthur said: "if you haven't got anything Mister Alleston then you have a drink with me", and put his hand in his pocket and gave Dad a shilling. The old man said: "Well I haven't had a drink in weeks" and got on his bike and pedalled down to Boxford to have one.

We hadn't got a penny, not two ha'ppenies, to rub together. We couldn't buy a penny stamp. I only had what I went out and earned and every day they took that off me one way or another, so I never had a penny. I might earn eight or ten shillings at night time. I had some good clients that I did hairdressing for, Lady Brunyet, she lived in the big house in Boxford, but the furthest I used to go was Great Horksley. It was the fourth parish from home. I used to leave Red House farm and go to Boxford, from Boxford to Polstead, from Polstead to Stoke by Nayland, Stoke by Nayland into Nayland, then Horksley. I used to do hair for Mrs Kerridge, the butcher's wife in Nayland. I had to go up that long old Horksley hill. You come to four cross roads at the top of that hill. That was more than a mile long. I never used to get there

until late 'cause I'd been to all these other places. She always used to make me a cup of cocoa before I came home and see that my lamp was lit on the front of my bike. If I had a puncture I would have had to walk. The only place that I was afraid was when I got to Polstead pond. When you got there, you had to go up a hill onto a road that had no houses for about a mile and a half. There was a high bank on the left hand side into Polstead Park and sometimes a deer would jump out of the park onto the road. I was always afraid I would see a deer up there, or that I might meet anybody when out late at night. I was always at the ready so if I met anybody or anything on that hill I should turn back downhill. That was the place where Maria Marten was murdered. I used to come all those miles alone. I went out every night. I went round Edwardstone and Groton and all those places on my little put-put bike.

I opened a hairdressing shop in Hadleigh but Dad still wouldn't leave me alone. Dad got somebody with a Ford pick up truck to take the milk straight from the cow house to Claydon. I was doing my hairdressing job and the rotten old bugger he had that chap come down with the truck and stop outside where I was hairdressing and waited for me to show him the way. I had to go with that man up to Ipswich with the milk. I said I wasn't going, I'd got my hairdressing to do, but I had to go. He'd have thrown me out if I hadn't gone. I only had the shop in Hadleigh for just over a month, I couldn't stand it. I said to Edna: "If you open a business at Hadleigh, you'll do all right", because I earned enough money to pay all my expenses and what they collected off me for sending the milk. Edna hired a room and eventually bought a place in George Street. She must have been about seventeen. Edna never looked back, but I was the one who started the business in Hadleigh. I continued at the farm.

When the wheat quota came in we sold the cows and ploughed

the land up again. I took the cows to market. We used the International tractor to plough the land. Hec Tricker learned to drive it as well. He lived in Brook Hall, he was Harry's nephew. Frank Tricker was our horseman, he also worked on the farm. He lived in the oblong cottages up the road next to Harry.

Edna invited me down there to tea. She was living down in Hadleigh now, where she started a shop. I had told her it would be a good idea to start a hairdressing shop. She was married at this time and had bought a house. She married Harold Bloomfield who was a baker's son and an apprentice engineer at Ransomes, Sims and Jeffries. It had a nice little garden at the back. It was Number Two George Street, Hadleigh. Anyway I went down there and there I met Arthur. I was invited down a fortnight before and had been told to be on my best behaviour. I called at Mary Kemball's and said I'm not going down there to be on 'my best behaviour' so I didn't go. A fortnight after she asked me down again, so I thought I'll go

and have a look at this bloke. I thought I'm not putting on best behaviour again, I don't care if I never see him again. This old country gal will shock him. Anyway I went and we had tea. I didn't shock him as he had been in the Navy and seen most things. We sat there talking and talking then I said: "Well I must be going". I had five miles to cycle home up Gallows Hill and past Kersey. Arthur said: "I'll come with you. I'll see you home". He came home with me and that was the beginning if our friendship.

We got married at Boxford Church 22 July 1935. All the people in the village were my friends, every one of them was my friend. They all called me by my Christian name and my sister who was younger than me, they called her Miss Alleston. Arthur used to say to me: "When are we going to get married?" because prior to that he had had an accident, and we had to put the wedding

Arthur while training at HMS Ganges, Shotley

off for about a year. He was injured internally. He had been riding his motorbike and he was flung up on some railings, because a farmer was silly enough to open a gate, go down to fetch his cows up and a freshly calved cow ran across the road when Arthur was passing and that was near Cundy's Gardens. It flung him up the road. Mr Cundy came along and Arthur had so much blood over his face and Mr Cundy had a new car and he wouldn't put him in his new car to take him to hospital in case he messed it up. The next person that came along was Bob somebody. He was manager of, or owned, the silk factory in Sudbury. He saw Arthur sitting on the side of the road all covered in blood. He said: "Get in boy. I'll take you to the hospital". Arthur got in and he took him to hospital and they found that, beside the abrasions on his head, he was injured internally which eventually caused his death eight years later. We should have been married that year but we weren't married 'cause they called me to the hospital to tell me that he was injured internally, so we waited 'til the next year. The next year we were going to be married and all the village were saying to me: "What day are you going to be married?" because they heard the banns asked and when the last banns were asked was on the Sunday and I said to Arthur that we'd get married on the Monday. The church warden and the bell ringer was a woman who lived opposite. She was the blacksmith's wife. Her name was Mrs Stone. Arthur went to her to say we wanted to get married quietly early on Monday morning, and please to not tell anybody. When it came to Monday morning, we arrived and of course there was nobody there, only the cousins from London. We were married but when we went in Mrs Stone had locked the church doors up so no one else could get in. When we looked round, there was all the faces at the church windows all looking in. The parson that married us said that he should take a leaf out of our book because you should never lock a church door. We went back up the farm and we had a cake. We cut the cake and we had our wedding breakfast at the farm. Arthur had as his best man a friend from out of the Navy. We left there and were going to Grandma and Grandpa Lanham's at Yarmouth because they couldn't get over to the wedding. We stayed there for a couple of nights at 70 Palgrave Road, then we were going to Portsmouth for our honeymoon, because he wanted to show me all round the Naval dockyards where he had been as a boy. When we got up there - I'm a bad car rider - I was sick twice going up to Yarmouth. I was better when I got there and soon recovered but Arthur was also ill and he went straight to bed when we got to his Mother and Father's. He was in bed for two or three days, so we never went to Portsmouth and never had our honeymoon.

George Lanham Snr, Arthur's father. He had sailed in the old sailing ships and was then coast guard at Great Yarmouth

So I was leaving the Red House and the old man said: "Will you sell me your horse, Nabs?". He knew how good she was and what she meant to me. So I drew up an agreement that Edna's husband Harold witnessed and let the old man have her at £25, which was for nothing. He couldn't pay and said that he would pay me when he received his first payment of the wheat quota about the end of January 1936. However he never did pay.

I was married eight years and out of those eight years he was never a well or fit man, he used to suffer with his liver. For the last two years, before he died, I pushed him around in a wheelchair.

I had left the farm in 1935 but the bad times continued there for a few more years. I was not there to help out although we went back continually most weekends and I had both my children christened at Boxford church. A year or two

A page from Emily's diary

RISES 7.54
SETS 4.30

JANUARY, 1939

MOON RISES 8.16 a.m. | 31 DAYS
MOON SETS 6.57 p.m. | 4TH WE

22 SUNDAY—3rd after Epiphany (22-343)

Neil was Christened at Boxford Church
Auntie, Joe, came down & Dad & Tets went home
with them =

23 MONDAY (23-342)

after I got married they had the fire over there. I was living at Earls Colne and I heard all about it.

Tickles woke up in the night. It was a very hot July time. There was lots of hay in the barn, there was also chaff. The men would go in there and have their lunch and a fag. It must have got very hot in there and all of a sudden the fire just burst out. Tickles woke up and saw the flames - realised what had happened, grabbed his trousers on and ran downstairs, let the greyhounds out as he went down, ran to the barn door where our stallion was but he was already down in his box. He was a beautiful horse. His name was Jolly he was a roan stallion - not so big as a Clydesdale but as big as a Shire. He was a lovely looking horse, he was a red roan - a strawberry roan. A gypsy, a travelling man, used to bring his mare every year to be covered by him. He used to pay Dad a pound. That mare had a foal every year, they were always strawberry roan like their father. He was furious when some people up the road said he had started that fire on purpose. He would not have lost that fine horse for anything. He thought the world of it. He was a kind horse too. I used to take him harrowing. A woman should never take a stallion out. They have a very keen sense of smell.

When the fire was raging in the barn, Kingsbury was up there, the builder. He said: " I expect you've

I owe upon Ruby Lanham the Sum of £25 — (twenty five) pounds for "habs

The conditions of Sale —

That the mare remains the property of Purchaser Charles Alleston and that. Ruby Lanham may ride and hunt the mare (when convenient to both Parties)

The £25 — to be paid when purchaser received his first Wheat Quota Cheque — about the end of January — signed ✗ Charles Alleston

witness by. Harold C. Bloomfield

December 1st — 1935.

got the place well insured Charles" and my father says: "No, I haven't, I never altered the insurance since when I bought it in 1902, never increased the insurance". The barn was only insured for £1,000. The barn and all those premises. The flames were going across to the apple tree which was outside the house and the firemen had to spray the house and he said: "You've got the house well insured then?" He said: "No, I've never altered the insurance on the house either". "Well" he said, "I couldn't build a house like yours today under three or four thousand pounds" and that was in the bad times. Dad had it insured for a few hundred. They brought all the things down and brought all the things out of the house and put them on the lawn but it never caught the house, thank God.

My father had got a mortgage on the farm and they wanted £1,000. Through the agricultural depression this person, Mrs Brown who was living in Devon had held the mortgage on the farm. Her solicitor wrote and said she was getting a very old lady and they would accept £1,000 to square the mortgage off which was a very good offer. My father had said he would accept it. When they had that fire, the barn was insured for £1000, but when the insurance people came round to value it, where the barn was built it was built, about two foot high on brick, then wood after the brick. Because those bricks still remained in position they wouldn't pay out the full £1000, they knocked £20 off but he paid off the mortgage.

Audrey with the thrashing team

The Government had to help the farmers somehow. So they promised that for every sack of wheat that was grown, they would pay a certain price. My father then put all the farm down to wheat, every inch, down to wheat. He thrashed it out and sold it and the next year he put all the farm down to wheat again. Wheat after wheat when he took the money for that, for the second lot. His luck seemed to change and just before the war he bought a drill. I think it was a Massey-Harris. It was one that drilled the corn and drilled the artificial manure together and he planted every acre with barley. Barley after wheat except for one field which he planted wheat after wheat, and he had an extraordinary good crop on that field. He grew all the rest of the farm with barley, drilled the barley with the artificial manure at the same time. He had an extraordinary good crop of barley, and he sold all his barley to Greene King at Bury and he took at one time a cheque for £7,000.00. He also had a load of clover when the price of clover seed went up about tenfold.

In the kitchen, where he had his desk in the corner, he used to pin cheques up on the wall. He had so many cheques he didn't know what to do with them all. Times changed completely when the war started. He didn't dare to put all his cheques in the bank. He didn't want to pay the income tax.

It was the year that they bought in a new tax system - farmers were going to be assessed. They had to pay so much tax for that year and they could grow all they wanted above that. They would not have to pay a higher tax the next year so this was the year of him being assessed and he had to keep his profit down.

Ru, Arthur, Audrey and Neil

He kept the barley late in the stack and the price kept going higher and higher and it had heated in the stack. It wasn't very good but they were so short of barley to make beer for the troops, they had to have it. There were all sorts of other cheques he had. He was now as rich as a sheeny. Because he did not want to have this high assessment he didn't know what to do with the money. He put £2,000 in Tickles' bank account and £2,000 in my mother's account as a gift. He went down to the bank and the bank manager said: "Well you've got a big deposit on here now Mr Alleston. What are you going to do with the money?" He said: "I've given £2,000 to my son and £2,000 to my wife".

The bank manager said: "Well can't you get rid of some more?

Dad said: "No, there's no one else I want to give any to" and the bank manager said: "What about your daughter, Ruby? She was a good help to you during the bad times".
"Well" he said: "She's married and got two children and her husband is dying of cancer".

The bank manager said: "Could you send £2,000 to a more deserving case?" and the old man sent £2,000 up to pay for Arthur to have an operation. By the time I got the cheque, he had had his operation and I had paid for it. So I had this cheque for £2,000 and Dad said: "Put it into your account then, but don't spend it". I put it into my banking account and every time I went home he asked me if I'd got that £2,000 intact. He wanted it back. He said: "You can spend your own money, but you can't spend that £2,000, because that's mine. You are just keeping it for me".

There was a house to be sold up the road called Elm Lodge and he said to me: "Ru, I'll have that £2,000 back now so I can buy Elm Lodge" I said: "I'd rather you didn't Dad, leave it where it is. I've kept it all this long time". "Have you ever broken into it?"
I said: "No. I've been down to my last pound, but I haven't broken into it" so he said: "I'll have it back and buy Elm Lodge and put it in your name". I said: "No thank-you Dad, I don't want Elm Lodge and I don't want it in my name, I'd rather keep the money". I refused to give him the £2,000 back to buy Elm Lodge and I'm very glad I did. I kept it because when he died, he never left me a penny not one iota.

The Maid of Oxford City

There once lived a maid in Oxford city, in Oxford city she did dwell
Was courted by a farmer's servant who oftimes vowed he loved her well

She loved him too but at a distance by or else she did not seem so fond
He said my dear you seem to slight me or else you love some other one

Or else my dear can't we get married and all at once be out of strife
I'll work for you both night and early if you'll be my true wedded wife

Not very long after this fair young damsel was invited to a ball you know
This jealous young man soon followed after and quickly he did overflow

He saw her dancing with another, a jealous thought came in his mind
He sought to destroy his own true lover this jealous young man he felt inclined

He then prepar'ed for some poison and mixed it with a glass of wine
He gave it to his own true lover who drank it with a willing mind

Not very long after this fair young damsel said take me home my dear said she
For that glass of wine you lately gave me has made me feel very ill said she

As they were walking home together this jealous young man to her did say
I put some poison in your wine dear to take your tender life away

And I have drank the same my jewel so I shall die as well as thee
In each others arms they died together fair maids beware of jealousy

Sung by Maria Johnson Windmill Hill, Glemsford who learned it
whilst working for Ropers in the weaving factory where they would
sing all day

Conclusion by Neil Lanham

Ruby's husband, Arthur, although he was ill for most of their marriage, received several promotions. His final one being as Area Manager of the Beds, Cambs and Hunts Electrical Company in St Neots, Huntingdonshire where he planned and estimated much of the lighting at local aerodromes. Arthur died on 12th December 1943. People said 'go back to your father, he will look after you' but Ruby had wintered and summered him and was not going to go down that route. Times were bad but she had seen hard times before. Through the war years when meat and clothing was on coupons, we lived on the things that most people didn't want. She would buy a gammon hock for a penny and make thick pea soup with marrowfat peas that would stand on the cooker for three days until the spoon stood up straight. We had tripe and onions, chitterlings, pork trotters, oxtail, stuffed sheep's heart. I went to school with sandwiches made of stuffed breast of mutton and homemade panyan pickle. Ruby sold her best modern furniture as it was then at a premium in the local auction and bought cheaper and then found she could sell this on for a profit so started dealing in furniture. She sublet the rooms in the chapel manse we rented and when served with notice to quit managed to get the incoming chapel minister to buy a big house up the road that she could rent. She had asked her father if she could spend the £2,000 of his that she had in her bank account on it and all he said was 'You'll not put any of my money in that!' The house had been derequisioned from the war department and was in a terrible state but here she scrubbed the floors and painted until she got one flat she could let, then another, then another, then another, even here she never lost her interest in horses and she always schemed a pony for us.

One day she said the best hunter judging in England is one stop from the railway station up the road, so she bundled us young children onto the train to go and watch the judging at the Peterborough Horse Show. She sat there and told us if a horse was roman nosed, lop eared, goose-rumped, long in the back, stifled or whatever there was to know about the horse she'd know. When a lady on horseback went round and a judge called her in and she didn't see it Ruby said she'd never come near a horse of mine. You go round with one eye on the judge at all times and when he looks at you a second time you don't wait to be called you take your horse in and if you think you've got a good chance you don't go in second place you go in front and let them put you down. Ruby knew about horses.

Wanting to get back to Suffolk she put her money down and borrowed the rest from the bank for a big house in Newmarket. Here she did the same as she did in St Neots and was soon out on the heath watching the horses. Her dream was to one day own a horse that would be good enough to win a race at Newmarket. Out on the heath in the early morning she met her old friend who was now Sir Alfred Munnings and President of the Royal Academy. He came and looked round her house as it had belonged to his friend, Frank Wellsman.

Up at Tattersalls auction one day she noticed a little foal who was lame come into the ring and thought that it had probably only been knocked in the box. On acquiring it at a maiden bid of 25 guineas she had it brought home where she cared for it. Rippatip, named after a song that the old man used to sing, went into training but did not win any races, Ruby had her covered as a mare and bred Obadiah. When Rippatip got a twisted gut and had to be put down Ruby said that it seemed to wait to see her to say goodbye and I imagined it did for animals seemed to respond to her, she spoke to them all the time, individually as though they were a person and an equal. Whilst out on the heath one day watching Rippatip training, she told the trainer that it was lame, "no that's not lame Mrs Lanham ha ha ha". A few minutes later he came back and said "you are right Mrs Lanham she is lame". At Huntingdon Races one day when a horse came down at the last fence Ruby knew instantly that it had broken its leg. As the horse tried to get up she shouted from the crowd 'sit on that horses head' for she knew the right thing to do was not to let it get up in that condition and the jockey duly went over and did as she bade him.

Ruby never forgot Boxford. Red House Farm was always referred to as 'home' and it seemed like it was for us children as that was where we spent all holidays and weekends when we could. She would often visit old Lazzie Pattle over by Groton Wood and it was a family ritual every Christmas morning to all walk over to Lazzie's with a Christmas pudding that Emily had made for him.

In later years Ruby had her mother come to live with us at Newmarket where she cared for her. In her final bedridden days a mouse got into the bedroom. They tried to catch it but had failed. Emily at this time was surviving on a few biscuits which she would munch when she felt like it and this the mouse knew. It would crawl up the bedpost and over the eiderdown and nibble the crumbs whilst she was dozing off to sleep. One time whilst she had a little piece of biscuit in her hand and was dozing she noticed out of the corner of her eye the mouse appearing and coming over the eiderdown. Although her hands were eaten up with rheumatism and her joints as big as footballs and she had a piece gone off one finger in a rat trap and the joint off another squashed where it had gone in a mangle, she still had enough nip left in her hand to kill that mouse when it got close enough. I think this story shows the necessity of the times that Ruby and her mother had been through. 'Needs be when the devil drives' said Ruby.

To the day she died she was frugal, she would never buy sliced ham but would wait until the last odd shaped piece at the end which the butcher would save for her for half a crown.

If you went to see her you never came away empty handed there would invariably be an apple turnover, a soused herring or two or better still a pork cheese that she had made from a pig's trotter. On a cold winter's day she would see the roadmen outside and ask him in for a cup of tea and put some whiskey in it to warm him up.

Obadiah fulfilled Ruby's lifelong dream on 2nd June 1984 by winning for her the Richard Marsh Handicap Stakes at Newmarket.

Charles Alleston died on the 5th October 1956 and is buried at Cuckoo Hill, Bures his home town. Emily Alleston died on the 7th February 1965 and is also buried at Cuckoo Hill, Bures. Ruby died on the 7th February 1998 and is buried at Kersey

Churchyard within the same parish as Red House Farm and where also lies her brothers Claude, Tickles and little Dick (in an unmarked grave somewhere near the church door).

These stories here were all told by Ruby at my request for the sake of story. They were for me to preserve and she knew that, she was telling them only for that purpose. Her stories however, were never brought out like that, they were all brought out from 'the back brain' when they were relevant to something in hand that had happened. They told what had happened in the past in similar circumstances to the present, they gave you something to go on, they were a measurement, they helped you to make a decision as to what was right now. They all had a principle of understanding, in short they passed wisdom. More important still they taught how to relate. The literate word for this is metaphor and I am convinced that in the present media dominated techno literate age it is something that we are all losing. We seem to have little time for story.

Ruby leadng Obadiah into the Winner's Enclosure after he had won for her the Richard Marsh Handicap Stakes at the Rowley Mile Course, Newmarket 2nd June 1984

Modern speech is full of information but all the information in the world is valueless if one cannot relate it. It is story that teaches one to relate and the ability to reason and that is the legacy that I feel I was left by my mother Ruby.

Ruby's speech

This is not intended to be a glossary of terms, far from it for that would be an attempt at a translation into standard English and I have tried hard to get away from such academic profile. I have tried to keep this book as an internal perspective and not an external one. An external perception comes when those of a purely literate background write about what is essentially and only an oral matter. There are many words that Ruby used that are listed in most such books that purport to represent the Suffolk dialect. Such observations by their nature tend to see little more than just words and sounds which is but a small part of the idiom of our speech. Far more important I feel and explicative are her metaphorical phrases for they give us a greater insight into the idiom of the people and most particularly the all important way that they think. I hope to expand on this in a later book, in the meantime here are a few of Ruby's words and sayings, that were all very much used by the local people at that time and a lot that tend not to be listed in those observations compiled by those of literate persuasion. Some are included in this book, some are not but all were used readily by herself or those around her. Many of them are not just names but metaphors and as such a reference to something from the past that puts a measured perspective on the situation in hand. A lot of these metaphorical sayings come from the horse and farming. Some could be made up through local every day occurrences such as 'hold my haddocks' (see page 24), others more general and could of course be used elsewhere, I do not purport to know. They are not peculiarities of speech for people of an external mindset to list because they are different from their standard English. These are our inheritance, are part of our identity and nothing other than the norm hereabout.

I list but a few (some of which have already been explained):

(he) drew him one off   He hit him
A tidy load   A fair size load
All of a white lather   Perspiring a lot like a horse

As right as a mailer	Absolutely correct
At that time of day	In that age
Barskuski	An exclamation of well being of Ruby's - I can only think that she got it from a comic - Pip Squeak and Wilfred's - Russian Auntie perhaps!
Been to the whist drive	Pregnant
Bread and pullet (it)	Plain bread (not chicken-a riddle)
Can't raise the wind	Can't find enough money
Cast in yer box	Can't get up in the morning - like a horse
Come hell or high water	I will prevail
Come in if yer good looking	Ruby always said this if someone knocked on her door. Unless she knew it was a stranger
Crabby	Irritable
Cupawee	The local command for a heavy horse to turn to the left
Dag	The morning dew
Dang	Damned
Don't you make a niase	Keep quiet about it (from Double Up Griggs)
Drive you shanny	Mad
Extracted his back teeth	Got the better of an individual in a deal
Fat as a teek	Fat
Fleet	To skim off cream
Fred Carnow's Circus	In a muddle (from a comic)
Freemans	For nothing
Gammy foot	Bad/lame
Getting a leg over	A horse will get it's leg over a ploughing trace
Going like helloa-ya	Going very fast
Wholly Sheenen	Going very fast - from the age of steam tackle machining
Wholly got the wick turned up	
	Going very fast
Grease the nail	Ruby would always grease a nail

	after it had gone through a hand or her foot
Hazeling	When the broken down tilth is just drying out and going crisp. Hazening in East Suffolk. It is still used orally by the people but I have not seen it in any of those books from the literate perspective.
His coat stare	Reference to a horse or dog that is in poor condition when its coat stands on end
His head don't ache now	He's been a long time dead
Hobbledehoy	Anyhow
Home 'treated'	A method of taking pork lard off the joint
Howsomever	However
I shall crack my jaw for no one	
	I shall not put a posh voice on
I was not born in a wood to be frightened of an owl	
	I don't scare easily
If I am alive and well (the good lord being willing)	
	a standard reservation when making a predictive statement
Joson Block	The mounting block that used to stand in the Red House farmyard, I am told the word originates from Jousting
Keep your tinder fan and lavel	
	Keep your fire in the steam engine fire box well spread
Kettlebaston Dockyard	A joke for Kettlebaston is well inland - it probably was once said of an old stackyard full of docks
Kisk	Brittle and frail ready to snap
Like the Corona Bus	Passengers inside - pregnant (a riddle)
Like the land of Goshen	A place that has everything
Lilly livered	Pathetic - no heart
Loblolly	A favourite of Ruby's mother - a useless person

Long headed man	A wise person
Long streak of pump water	To talk disparagingly of a tall, thin person
Lu, lu, lu, lu, lu	The sound you teach your dog to recognise when a hare or rabbit gets up
Nabbed the rust	Took offence
Nappy	A temperamental horse that will stop
Needs be when the devil drives	When necessity demands
Never have it said boy yer mother bred a jibber	You must play your part
No bumming	The truth (from Double Up Griggs)
No go to or come from	Background unknown - no identity
No great shakes	Not very good
Not a mucher	Not very good
Oh be joyful	A heart warming spirit of the liquid sort!
Poisoned of money (or rats)	Very rich - over run
Put that door to	Close that door
Queech	The Queech (or Creach) ran along the bottom of racecourse field and was and still is a deep ditch. Possibly dialect of Creek?
Red house farm stands on a dog leg	A right angle bend
Rich as a sheeny	Very well off
Riding habit	A long high waisted flared coat used for hunting
Sare	Dry and tinderful
Scotchmen	Big sow thistles in the corn
She-nan-okin	Playing the fool
Sludder	A thick puddingy mud
Smetick	The tiniest part
Stovver	Hay from the Clover crop
Tender as a boiled owl	Tough

Thank yer mother for the eggs

Goodbye - good to see you

That cut out his chortling in church

Cut down to size

The brew
The very edge of a field before the ditch

The wherewith all
The ability to - could be money

They'd lick the whitening off the wall

Very mean

They wouldn't give you the time of day

Very mean

They'll lift yer leg
Take advantage of you

To be in someone ribs
In debt to them

To crab something
To complain and talk down about it

To have a dog tied up
An unpaid bill

To tight up
To tidy up

Tow
A fluffy by product of flax

Wardee
The local command for a heavy horse to turn to the right. Interesting because Ruby sang it in the song at the start of chapter five - its only found in mid / east Suffolk.

We had enough of his pielar (buck)

Messing about

Wellum
A ditch beside a gateway

Were you born in a barn?
Please close the door that you left open

Wher-up bor
Hello mate - a standard greeting

Wid
A horse with its wind gone

Worn to a frazzle
Worn nearly away

You have to winter and summer them

Take your time to understand

You neither come nigh me or by me

You didn't come to see me

You've got your feet well under the table there

You are well in

A DVD of the Narrative

RUBY AND HER HORSES
recorded live at Felsham Village Hall on 18th
February 2006 including many of Ruby's stories from
this book told by Neil Lanham and ten specially
composed songs sung by Andrew Stanard is
available priced £12.95 including postage.

A CD of the
singing tradition of the people of Lavenham
and its surrounding area including many songs
mentioned herein from the Voices of Ruby, Sidney
Turkentine, Arthur Balaam, Sid Hollicks, Ria Johnson
and Alby Avenue from Kettlebaston Dockyard is
available. Price £10.50 including postage.
This is one of 12 CDs in the Voice of Suffolk Series
and a list of these and other DVDs including stories
from traditional horsemen, stallion walkers,
gamekeepers, steam engine drivers etc is available
from:

Neil Lanham,
The Helions Bumpstead Gramophone Co,
Ivy Todd, Helions Bumpstead, Nr Haverhill, Suffolk,
CB9 7AT
Tel. 01440 730414. Also see
www.traditionsofsuffolk.com

Rear cover: Ru on the unique Pedal Roller by ASF Robinson that came from Letts Sale at the Hollies